Nuclear Proliferation
Risk and Responsibility

A Report to
The Trilateral Commission

Foreword by
HENRY A. KISSINGER

North American Author
GRAHAM ALLISON

European Authors
HERVÉ DE CARMOY
THÉRÈSE DELPECH

Pacific Asian Author
CHUNG MIN LEE

Comment by
PIERRE GOLDSCHMIDT

Published by
The Trilateral Commission
Washington, Paris, Tokyo
2006

Library of Congress Cataloging-in-Publication Data

Nuclear proliferation : risk and responsibility : a report to the Trilateral Commission / foreword, Henry A. Kissinger ; authors, Graham Allison ... [et al.] ; comment, Pierre Goldschmidt.
    p. cm.
Includes bibliographical references.
ISBN-10: 0-930503-88-0
ISBN-13: 978-0-930503-88-8
1. Nuclear nonproliferation. 2. Nuclear weapons--Iran. 3. Nuclear weapons--Korea (North) I. Allison, Graham T. II. Trilateral Commission.
JZ5675.N8383 2006
  --dc22

          2006028986

The Trilateral Commission

www.trilateral.org

1156 15th Street, NW
Washington, DC 20005

5, Rue de Téhéran
75008 Paris, France

Japan Center for International Exchange
4-9-17 Minami-Azabu
Minato-ku
Tokyo 106, Japan

Contents

Foreword

There is no greater challenge to the global nuclear order today than the impending proliferation of nuclear weapons and the increasing likelihood that terrorists may conduct a nuclear 9/11, devastating one of the great cities of the world. The papers presented in this report from the Trilateral Commission's 2006 annual meeting in Tokyo offer a comprehensive and insightful overview of this urgent challenge.

During the Cold War, a balance of terror was precariously maintained between the two superpowers. Leaders of both knew that their first imperative was to avoid a nuclear Armageddon, of which both would be the first victim. Even then, the disparity between the vast consequences of a decision to use nuclear weapons on the one hand and any conceivable political outcome that could be achieved on the other hand had a paralyzing effect on decision making. The deliberate choice to use nuclear weapons in a preventive or preemptive manner defied the principles of rational conduct, since it guaranteed casualties among the civilian populations of both superpowers that were beyond comprehension.

If one imagines a world of tens of nations with nuclear weapons and major powers trying to balance their own deterrent equations, plus the deterrent equations of the subsystems, deterrence calculation would become impossibly complicated. To assume that, in such a world, nuclear catastrophe could be avoided would be unrealistic.

As the world's unmatched military superpower, the United States has a unique role in preventing the spread of nuclear weapons. The Bush administration's National Security Strategy explicitly warns that "there are few greater threats than a terrorist attack with WMD" and that "the greater the threat, the greater is the risk of inaction-and the more compelling the case for taking anticipatory action to defend ourselves, even if uncertainty remains as to the time and place of the enemy's attack."

But a preemptive strategy for using force to deny the spread of nuclear weapons is based on assumptions that cannot be proved when they are made. When the scope for action is greatest, knowledge is at a minimum. When knowledge has been acquired, the scope for preemption has often disappeared.

The tension, therefore, is between preemptive and preventive uses of force. Preemption applies to an adversary possessing a capacity to do great, potentially irreversible, damage, coupled with the demonstrated will to do so imminently. The right to use force unilaterally in such circumstances has been accepted for centuries.

Preventive uses of force are measures to forestall the emergence of a threat not yet imminent, but capable, at some point in the future, of being potentially overwhelming. Preventive force is not an issue applicable to relations with an established major nuclear adversary. First-strike threats against established nuclear powers might, if such powers felt their weapons were very vulnerable, tempt them to make a preemptive strike of their own. A policy of using preventive force against aspiring nuclear powers, however, creates incentives for them to acquire nuclear weapons as rapidly as possible and, if thwarted, to develop chemical or biological weapons-either for their own security or as a safety net for assertive or revolutionary policies.

All major powers have a responsibility to take the challenge of preventing nuclear proliferation seriously. A common approach may be possible because what used to be called the "great powers" have nothing to gain by military conflict with each other. They are all dependent on the global economic system. They should recognize that, after the explosion of just one nuclear bomb in one of their great cities, their publics will demand an extreme form of preventive diplomacy to assure that this can never happen again. Without waiting for such a catastrophe, statesmen should now be building a viable international order that will prevent such nightmares from ever occurring.

As the papers in this report argue persuasively, the entire nonproliferation regime is now at risk. North Korea and Iran threaten to become nuclear weapons states. Osama bin Laden seeks nuclear weapons to realize his stated goal of killing millions of American citizens. At the conclusion of a most productive discussion of the Tokyo meeting, members of the Commission were united in the hope that this report will spur all our governments to greater urgency in combating this grave and growing threat.

Henry A. Kissinger
August 24, 2006

The Authors

Graham Allison is Douglas Dillon Professor of Government and director of the Belfer Center for Science and International Affairs at Harvard's John F. Kennedy School of Government. Dr. Allison's latest book, *Nuclear Terrorism: the Ultimate Preventable Catastrophe*, was selected by the *New York Times* as one of the "100 Notable Books of 2004." From 1977 to 1989, Dr. Allison served as dean of the Kennedy School. Under his leadership, a small, undefined program grew 20-fold to become a major professional school of public policy and government. Dr. Allison served as special adviser to the secretary of defense under President Reagan and as assistant secretary of defense under President Clinton. He has twice been awarded the Defense Department's highest honor for civilians, the Distinguished Public Service Medal, most recently for "reshaping relations with Russia, Ukraine, Belarus, and Kazakhstan to reduce the former Soviet nuclear arsenal."

Dr. Allison has authored or coauthored more than a dozen books and hundreds of articles, including *Realizing Human Rights: From Inspiration to Impact* (2000); *Avoiding Nuclear Anarchy: Containing the Threat of Loose Russian Nuclear Weapons and Fissile Material* (1996); *Cooperative Denuclearization: From Pledges to Deeds* (1993); and *Beyond Cold War to Trilateral Cooperation in the Asia-Pacific Region* (1992). His first book, *Essence of Decision: Explaining the Cuban Missile Crisis* (1971), released in an updated and revised second edition (1999), ranks among the best sellers in political science, with more than 400,000 copies in print.

Dr. Allison has been a member of the secretary of defense's Defense Policy Board for secretaries Weinberger, Carlucci, Cheney, Aspin, Perry and Cohen. Dr. Allison was a founding member of the Trilateral Commission, a director of the Council on Foreign Relations, and a member of many public committees and commissions. He has served on the boards of the Getty Oil Company, New England Securities, The Taubman Companies, and Belco Oil and Gas, as well as on the advisory boards of Chase Bank, Hydro-Quebec, and the International Energy Corporation. He was educated at Davidson College, earned a bachelor's degree in history at Harvard College; a bachelor's degree and a master's degree in philosophy, politics, and economics at Oxford University; and his doctoral degree at Harvard University.

Hervé de Carmoy is currently chairman of Almatis (formerly Alcoa Specialty Chemicals), a majority-owned company by Rhône Group LLC, in Frankfurt-am-Main. From 1998 to 2004, he was a partner of the Rhône Group LLC in New York and Paris. Prior his position with the Rhône Group, he was chairman of the Banque Industrielle Mobilière et Privée (BIMP) and adviser to the chairman of HR Finances in Paris. Educated at l'Institut d'Études Politiques in Paris and at Cornell University in the United States, he began his career at the Chase Manhattan Bank in 1963 and became its director for Europe in 1973. After joining Midland Bank in 1978, Mr. de Carmoy became director and chief executive international, London and Paris, and chairman of Thomas Cook, a position he held until 1988. He was then chief executive of Société Générale de Belgique in Brussels until February 1991.

An author, Mr. de Carmoy was also a Trilateral Commission task force author of *Restoring Growth in the Debt-Laden Third World* (1987, with Martin Feldstein and Koei Narusawa). He was elected European deputy chairman of the Trilateral Commission in 2004 and served as chairman of the French Group of the Commission.

Thérèse Delpech is currently director of strategic affairs at the French Atomic Energy Commission and senior research fellow at the Center for International Studies (CERI—Fondation Nationale des Sciences Politiques), Paris. She was also UNMOVIC commissioner, member of the IISS Council, and member of the international Commission on Weapons of Mass Destruction chaired by Hans Blix. She chaired the UN Advisory Board for Disarmament Matters in 1999. She also served as adviser to the French prime minister, Alain Juppé, for politico-military affairs (1995–97). Most of her career has been at the service of the Atomic Energy Commission of France, where she served as deputy director, International Affairs Division, and as adviser to the high commissioner. She has also served as permanent consultant to the Policy Planning Staff, Ministry of Foreign Affairs (1991–95).

She is the author of three books: *L'Héritage nucléaire* (Complexe, 1997), *La Guerre Parfaite* (Flammarion, 1998) and *Politique du Chaos* (Le Seuil, 2002), and numerous articles in *Politique Etrangère, Internationale Politik, Survival, Global, Commentaire, Politique Internationale, Cahiers de Chaillot* on the subject of nuclear issues, weapons of mass destruction, and strategic issues. Thérèse Delpech has published recently *L'Ensauvagement: le retour de la Barbarie au XXIème siècle* (Grasset, 2006).

Henry Alfred Kissinger was sworn in on September 22, 1973, as the 56th secretary of state, a position he held until January 20, 1977. He also served as assistant to the president for national security affairs from January 20, 1969, until November 3, 1975. In July 1983 he was appointed by President Ronald Reagan to chair the National Bipartisan Commission on Central America until it ceased operation in January 1985, and from 1984 to 1990 he served as a member of the President's Foreign Intelligence Advisory Board. From 1986 to 1988 he was a member of the Commission on Integrated Long-Term Strategy of the National Security Council and Defense Department. He is currently a member of the Defense Policy Board.

At present, Dr. Kissinger is chairman of Kissinger Associates, Inc., an international consulting firm. He is also a member of the International Council of J. P. Morgan Chase & Co.; chairman of the International Advisory Board of American International Group, Inc.; a counselor to and trustee of the Center for Strategic and International Studies; an honorary governor of the Foreign Policy Association; and an honor member of the International Olympic Committee. Among his other activities, Dr. Kissinger is a member of the board of directors of ContiGroup Companies, Inc., and a public sector member of the United States Olympic Committee. He is also an adviser to the board of directors of American Express Company; a member of the advisory board of Forstmann Little and Co.; a trustee emeritus of the Metropolitan Museum of Art; a director emeritus of Freeport-McMoRan Copper and Gold Inc.; and a director of the International Rescue Committee. Among the awards Dr. Kissinger has received have been the Nobel Peace Prize in 1973; the Presidential Medal of Freedom (the nation's highest civilian award) in 1977; and the Medal of Liberty (given one time to ten foreign-born American leaders) in 1986.

Dr. Kissinger was born in Fürth, Germany, came to the United States in 1938, and was naturalized a United States citizen in 1943. He served in the U.S. Army from 1943 to 1946. He graduated summa cum laude from Harvard College and received master's degree and a doctoral degree from Harvard University. From 1954 until 1969 he was a member of the faculty of Harvard University, in both the department of government and the Center for International Affairs. He was director of the Harvard International Seminar from 1952 to 1969. Dr. Kissinger is the author of numerous books, including *Nuclear Weapons and Foreign Policy* (1957); *White House Years* (1979); *Does America Need a Foreign*

Policy?: Toward a Diplomacy for the 21ˢᵗ Century (2001); *Ending the Vietnam War: A History of America's Involvement in and Extrication from the Vietnam War* (2003); and *Crisis: The Anatomy of Two Major Foreign Policy Crises* (2003). He has also published numerous articles on U.S. foreign policy, international affairs, and diplomatic history. His column, syndicated by Tribune Media Services International, appears in leading U.S. newspapers and in more than 40 foreign countries.

Chung Min Lee is a visiting professor at the Lee Kuan Yew School of Public Policy, National University of Singapore. He has written widely on East Asian security, threat assessment, defense planning dynamics, and the proliferation of weapons of mass destruction. His current research interests include East Asian security and defense, risk assessment, and leadership profiles. A graduate of the political science department at Yonsei University, he received his master's degree and doctoral degree from the Fletcher School of Law and Diplomacy, Tufts University. Currently on leave from the National Graduate Institute for Policy Studies, Yonsei University, Seoul, Dr. Lee was at the National Graduate Institute for Policy Studies, Tokyo, from September 2004 until September 2005. Before joining the Lee Kuan Yew School, Dr. Lee was a policy analyst at RAND (1995–98), a visiting fellow at the National Institute for Defense Studies, Tokyo (1994–95), a research fellow at the Sejong Institute (1989–94), a research fellow at the Institute of East and West Studies, Yonsei University (1988–89), and a research fellow at the Institute for Foreign Policy Analysis, Cambridge, Mass. (1985–88).

Dr. Lee is currently a member of the Advisory Committee, Ministry of Foreign Affairs and Trade; the National Emergency Planning Commission; and the Republic of Korea Air Force. He has also served as an adviser to the Republic of Korea National Security Council Secretariat (1999–2001). He is a member of the International Institute for Strategic Studies (London) and the Seoul Forum for International Affairs (SFIA).

1

Global Challenges
of Nuclear Proliferation

Graham Allison

The topic of this Trilateral Report is truly a moving target. As we meet,[1] North Korea has reprocessed enough plutonium for eight nuclear bombs, restarted its Yongbyon reactor where it is producing enough plutonium for two additional bombs a year, and has thus crossed a line President Bush has repeatedly declared would be "intolerable." Defying the UN Security Council's demand that it suspend uranium enrichment-related activity at Isfahan and Natanz, Iran is accelerating its program and making threats to "wipe Israel off the map." The United States has agreed unilaterally to provide civilian nuclear technology and nuclear fuel to India, an agreement that still requires Congress to amend the U.S. Atomic Energy Act, and its international partners in the Nuclear Suppliers Group to accept India's special status as a nuclear weapons state. The subject of our report is thus moving—not like a train on a track, but rather like quicksilver that quivers and darts, often in unpredictable directions.

The question is: How do the developments we are now witnessing impact the vital national interests of the Trilateral countries? It is fitting that we consider this question in Japan, the only state to have been the target of a nuclear attack. Indeed, it is appropriate to pause and reflect on the devastation caused by U.S. atomic bombs dropping on Hiroshima and Nagasaki 60 years ago.

How do current developments impact Trilateralists' vital national interests? The answer is that they affect their interests hugely—perhaps even fatally.

In April 2006, two days after stepping down from 13 years at the helm of the *Economist*, Bill Emmott was my guest at a special event at Harvard. As is the tradition at the *Economist*, as his final act, the editor

---

[1] Trilateral Commission 2006 Annual Meeting, April 22–24, Tokyo.

writes a substantial review of developments in the world during his tenure. Bill's essay appeared on April 2. In that review, he notes the unbelievable pace and extent of globalization that has occurred over the last 13 years. As he looks to the future, his best forecast is faster and deeper globalization. But in conclusion, he asks: What could upset that forecast and even reverse the trend? His answer: a single nuclear bomb exploding in any capital in the world.

American President Harry Truman's secretary of state, Dean Acheson, entitled his memoir *Present at the Creation*. He describes elegantly the post–World War II creation of the United Nations, the IMF, the World Bank, NATO, the U.S.-Japan Defense Treaty, and the Marshall Plan that reconstructed Europe and Japan and established a new international order rightly entitled the "free world." The fundamental question Trilateralists must confront as we meet to consider nuclear proliferation and terrorism today is whether we are present at the unraveling of the nonproliferation regime that has held back the spread of nuclear weapons. Are we witnessing the end of nuclear restraint and the beginning of the nightmare President John F. Kennedy warned about four decades ago?

Recall President Kennedy's famous prediction in 1962 that "by 1970 there may be 10 nuclear powers instead of 4, and by 1975, 15 or 20." Had nations created nuclear arsenals as soon as they acquired the advanced technical capability to do so, Kennedy's prediction would have proved correct. But his warning helped awaken the world to the unacceptable dangers of unconstrained nuclear proliferation. The world refused to accept the consequences of those projections, and instead negotiated international constraints, the centerpiece of which is the Treaty on the Non-Proliferation of Nuclear Weapons (NPT). The NPT offers a bargain: the five original nuclear weapons states pledge to disarm and swear not to transfer nuclear weapons to others, while the nonnuclear weapons states receive the benefits of peaceful nuclear technology and commit not to build or acquire nuclear bombs. Over time, export control regimes, interdiction organizations, and nuclear weapons–free zones have fleshed out the nonproliferation regime.

Thanks to that regime, today 183 nations, including scores that have the technical capability to build nuclear arsenals, have renounced nuclear weapons. Four decades later, there are only 8-1/2 nuclear weapons states, not 20 or 40 (figure 1.1). Moreover, despite moments of risk— most dangerously the Cuban Missile Crisis of 1962 but more recently

Figure 1.1. The Nuclear Age, 1939–2005

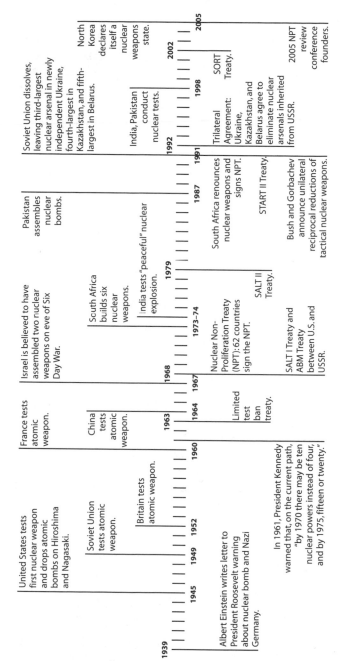

Source: Research by the author.

Note: Argentina, Australia, Brazil, Canada, Egypt, Germany, Greece, Indonesia, Iraq, Italy, Japan, Libya, Romania, South Korea, Sweden, Switzerland, Taiwan, Turkey, and Yugoslavia all pursued nuclear weapons programs but abandoned them.

the Indian-Pakistani confrontation of 2002—no nuclear weapon has been used in an attack on an adversary for 60 years.

As Henry Kissinger has noted, a defining challenge for statesmen is to recognize "a change in the international environment so likely to undermine national security that it must be resisted no matter what form the threat takes or how ostensibly legitimate it appears." Iran's and North Korea's emergence as nuclear weapons states would constitute just such a transformation for the nations of the Trilateral community. The question is whether their statesmen will act in time to prevent this outcome.

This report to the Trilateral Commission begins with an overview of the global challenge of nuclear nonproliferation and nuclear terrorism from a U.S. perspective. European authors, Hervé de Carmoy and Thérèse Delpech, then present from a European standpoint the Iranian case study. Finally, Chung Min Lee offers an Asian view on the North Korean challenge.

A North American Perspective: Executive Summary

Let me begin by stating starkly, and provocatively, three central conclusions.

First, the single most serious threat to the national security of the Trilateral countries (and the world) is nuclear terrorism—the devastation of one of the world's great cities by a terrorist nuclear bomb. In the hotly contested U.S. presidential election of 2004, the two candidates agreed on only one fundamental point. In the first televised debate, they were asked, what is "the single greatest threat to American national security?" Senator Kerry answered: nuclear terrorism. President Bush said, "I agree with my opponent that the biggest threat facing the country is weapons of mass destruction (WMD) in the hands of a terrorist network."

The other Trilateral countries face the same threat. Nobel Prize winner Mohamed ElBaradei has warned, "The threat of nuclear terrorism is real and current." As UN Secretary General Kofi Annan has noted:

> Nuclear terrorism is still often treated as science fiction. I
> wish it were. But unfortunately we live in a world of excess
> hazardous materials and abundant technological know-how,
> in which some terrorists clearly state their intention to inflict

catastrophic casualties . . . Were a nuclear terrorist attack to occur, it would cause not only widespread death and destruction, but would stagger the world economy and thrust tens of millions of people into dire poverty.

How likely is such a catastrophe? Risk equals probability times consequences. Thus, even skeptics who believe that experts overestimate the probability find it difficult to discount the risk.

Second, the nonproliferation regime is today precariously poised at a tipping point. The UN's Weapons of Mass Destruction Commission laments that "global treaties . . . constituted insufficient barriers against the efforts of Iraq, North Korea and Libya to acquire nuclear weapons and against Iran to conceal a programme for the enrichment of uranium." As the international high-level panel of wise men and women commissioned by the UN to review threats to global security concluded: the most serious threat to international peace and security is the "erosion of the nonproliferation regime" to a point that "could become irreversible and result in a cascade of proliferation."

Third, this ultimate catastrophe for each of our countries and the world is preventable. There exists a feasible, affordable agenda of actions that the nations of the world could take to reduce to nearly zero the likelihood of a terrorist's Hiroshima. But current trend lines are going in the opposite direction—indeed, heading toward predictable catastrophe. Preventing nuclear terrorism will thus require a significant departure from current behavior.

Nuclear Dangers Today

After Hiroshima and Nagasaki, the specter that haunted the twentieth century was a nuclear mushroom cloud. The face of nuclear danger today is a nuclear 9/11. As former Mexican president Ernesto Zedillo has observed:

We all should have a pretty clear idea of what would follow a nuclear weapon's detonation in any of the world's major cities . . . The loss of life could be in the hundreds of thousands (if not millions), the destruction of property in the trillions of dollars, the escalation in conflicts and violence uncontrollable, the erosion of authority and government unstoppable and the disruption of global trade and finance unprecedented. In short, we could practically count on the beginning of another dark age.

For Trilateralists old enough to remember the Cold War, this may seem like "déjà vu all over again." Because nuclear weapons lay at the heart of that great struggle, many regard it as unfair that this threat was not buried with that era. But the brute fact is that the old arsenals of that war did not disappear with it. The United States and Russia still possess nearly 30,000 nuclear warheads and hundreds of thousands of weapons' worth of fissile material—material with a half-life of at least 24,000 years. In addition, the nuclear community faces the problem of "new nukes": India and Pakistan have emerged as de facto nuclear weapons states, and North Korea and Iran lead the pack of "nuclear wannabes."

In a post-9/11 world, traditional Cold War policies of deterrence and containment are no longer sufcient. Deterrence, which discouraged other states from launching a nuclear attack on the United States through the threat of overwhelming retaliation, is less applicable to suicide bombers or terrorists with no return address.

How real is the threat of terrorists exploding a nuclear bomb and devastating a great metropolis? In the judgment of former U.S. senator Sam Nunn, the likelihood of a single nuclear bomb exploding in a single city is greater today than at the height of the Cold War. *Nuclear Terrorism* states my own judgment that, on the current trend line, the chances of a nuclear terrorist attack in the next decade are greater than 50 percent.[2] Former secretary of defense William Perry has expressed his own view that *Nuclear Terrorism* underestimates the risk. According to the world's most successful investor, Warren Buffet, a nuclear terrorist attack "will happen. It's inevitable. I don't see any way that it won't happen." Companies who sell "catastrophic terrorism insurance" exclude nuclear attack from their policies. Otherwise these insurance companies would be "vulnerable to extinction," in Buffett's words.

To assess the threat of nuclear terrorism, it is necessary to answer five questions.[3]

---

2 Graham Allison. *Nuclear Terrorism: The Ultimate Preventable Catastrophe* (New York: Times Books, 2004; Tokyo, Nihon Keizai Shimbun, 2006).

3 These five questions are the titles of the first five chapters of *Nuclear Terrorism*.

1. Who could be planning a nuclear terrorist attack? Al Qaeda remains a formidable enemy with clear nuclear ambitions. The former head of the CIA's Bin Laden task force, Michael Scheuer, has detailed how, in May 2003, Bin Laden acquired a fatwa from a Saudi cleric providing a religious justification to use nuclear weapons against the United States. Entitled "A Treatise on the Legal Status of Using Weapons of Mass Destruction Against Infidels," it asserts that "if a bomb that killed 10 million of them and burned as much of their land as they have burned Muslims' land were dropped on them, it would be permissible." Scheuer, who followed terrorism and militant Islam for much of his 22-year career, is particularly troubled by "the careful, professional manner in which al Qaeda was seeking to acquire nuclear weapons."

But the threats do not stop at Al Qaeda. Europe's 15 million Arabs and Muslims are four times as likely to be unemployed as native Europeans. Many feel humiliated and alienated, and they see little chance for assimilation. The Madrid attacks in 2004 revealed an explosive cocktail that mixed foreign terrorists, disaffected locals, and organized crime. London's 7/7 subway bombers appear to have been home-grown. Recall the stark warning left on the body of the murdered Dutch filmmaker, Theo van Gogh: "I know definitely that you, Oh Europe, will go down."

In 1995, Tokyo found itself the target of cult members wielding the first large-scale chemical weapons attack on a civilian population. Aum Shinrikyo aimed to kill large numbers and eventually overthrow the government of Japan. The sect was also seeking nuclear weapons.

2. What nuclear weapons could terrorists use? Terrorists could acquire a bomb in one of two ways: by obtaining a ready-made weapon from the arsenal of one of the nuclear weapons states or by constructing an elementary nuclear bomb from highly enriched uranium (HEU) made by a state. Theft of a warhead by insiders, or a combination of insiders and intruders, would not be easy. But attempted thefts in Russia and elsewhere are not uncommon.

In 1993, Captain Alexei Tikhomirov of the Russian navy entered the Sevmorput shipyard near Murmansk through an unguarded gate, broke into a building used to store nuclear submarine fuel, and stole three pieces of a reactor core containing about 10 pounds of HEU. He put the fuel in a bag and then walked out of the shipyard the way he came in. Tikhomirov was arrested eight months later when he sought help selling the material. His asking price was $50,000. The lead Russian prosecutor in the case noted that "potatoes were guarded better" than the nuclear fuel at Murmansk.[4] Although security at Russian nuclear facilities has increased dramatically since the early 1990s, as of 2004, only 26 percent of former Soviet nuclear materials had received comprehensive security upgrades.[5]

In 2004, Chechen guerrilla forces demonstrated yet again their organizational capacity to seize facilities inside Russia as well as their readiness to murder ruthlessly—this time killing 186 Beslan schoolchildren. On the first day of the hostage crisis, President Vladimir Putin dispatched additional troops to guard Russia's undersecured nuclear facilities. Whatever the security at these facilities was the day before the school seizure, Putin understood that it was inadequate the day after. Immediately following the hostage taking, Putin proclaimed, "We are dealing with the direct intervention of international terror against Russia with total and full-scale war." But despite Putin's initial response to Beslan, the follow-up lags.

Once a terrorist group acquires 100 pounds of HEU, building an elementary nuclear bomb no longer takes the mind of an Oppenheimer, or even an A. Q. Khan. Standing on these shoulders, with fissile material acquired from a weapons state, using publicly available documents and items commercially obtainable in any technologically advanced country, terrorists could construct a gun-type bomb like the one dropped on Hiroshima.

3. Where could terrorists acquire a nuclear bomb? If a nuclear terrorist attack occurs, Russia will be the most likely source of the weapon or material—not because the Russian government would intentionally sell or lose them, but simply because Russia's 11-time-zone expanse contains more nuclear weapons and materials than any other country in the world, much of it still vulnerable to theft. A close second, A. Q. Khan, the father of Pakistan's nuclear bomb, was also— simultaneously—the world's first nuclear black marketer. As evidence from Libya has revealed, A. Q. Khan directed a global supply network selling centrifuges for enriching nuclear material, uranium hexafluoride in quantities necessary for a nuclear bomb (most likely from North

---

4 Oleg Bukharin and William Potter, "Potatoes Were Guarded Better," *Bulletin of Atomic Scientists* (May–June 1995).

5 Matt Bunn and Anthony Wier, "Securing the Bomb: The New Global Imperative," www.nti.org/cnwm.

Korea), nuclear warhead designs (from China), and consulting services to help assemble the pieces. As the director of the International Atomic Energy Agency (IAEA) observed, A. Q. Khan was running a "Wal-Mart of private-sector proliferation." In addition, research reactors in 40 developing and transitional countries still hold the essential ingredient for nuclear bombs.

4. When could terrorists launch the first nuclear attack? If terrorists bought or stole a nuclear weapon in good working condition, they could explode it today. If the weapon had a lock, the date of detonation would be delayed for several days. If terrorists acquired the 100 pounds of HEU needed for an elementary nuclear bomb, they could have a working bomb in less than a year.

5. How could terrorists deliver a nuclear weapon to its target? Two plausible methods would be to "follow the golf clubs" and "follow the drugs."

Imagine a woman who lives in Tokyo, wants to play golf in Pebble Beach, but prefers to avoid the hassle of carrying her clubs through U.S. customs. How would she get her clubs to the resort? She would call up a freight forwarder, provide a plausible description of the contents of her shipment, and have her golf bag picked up at her home. The clubs would travel by ship from Tokyo to the Port of Oakland and then by truck to the golf course. The chance of anyone inspecting her bag between her house and the links is less than 3 percent.

If that seems too risky, terrorists might "follow the drugs," tons of which find their way to U.S. cities every day. The illicit economy for narcotics and illegal immigrants has built up a vast infrastructure that terrorists could exploit. As a former colleague of mine has noted, no one should doubt the ability of terrorists to bring a nuclear weapon to New York; they could simply hide it in a bale of marijuana, which we know comes to all global cities.

Lest this seem too hypothetical or theoretical, reflect on an actual incident that occurred in the United States one month to the day after the 9/11 attacks on the World Trade Center and Pentagon. A CIA agent, code-named Dragonfire, reported that Al Qaeda had acquired a live nuclear weapon produced by the former Soviet Union and had successfully smuggled it into New York City. A top-secret team was dispatched to the city to search for a nuclear bomb. Under a cloak of secrecy that excluded even Mayor Rudolph Giuliani, Nuclear Emergency

Search Teams began a hunt for the 10-kiloton bomb whose Hiroshima-sized blast could have obliterated a significant portion of Manhattan.

Fortunately, Dragonfire's report turned out to be a false alarm. But the threat was credible for good reasons. Did former Soviet stockpiles include a large number of 10-kiloton weapons? Yes. Could the Russian government account for all its nuclear bombs? No. Could Al Qaeda have acquired one? Yes. Could it have smuggled a nuclear weapon through border controls and into a U.S. city? Certainly. The takeaway truth is this: the U.S. government had no grounds in science or in logic to dismiss the warning. If the Japanese, French, or German government received such a warning today, it would also have to take the threat seriously.

Nonproliferation Regime Eroding

In preparing for the 60th anniversary of the United Nations, Secretary General Kofi Annan established a panel of leading thinkers to assess global threats to the world's population, now over 6.5 billion people, in the quarter century ahead. In an unusually thoughtful and provocative report, the panel identified six principal threats from poverty to environmental degradation. But among the threats, the commission gave primacy of place to renewed nuclear danger driven by the proliferation of nuclear weapons and the possibility of nuclear terrorist attacks. As noted above, the panel warned starkly that the nonproliferation regime had eroded to the point of "irreversibility" that could trigger a "cascade of proliferation."

How might such a catastrophic cascade occur? Simply by continuing on the trend line of the past decade. On their current trajectories, North Korea and Iran will become nuclear weapons states before the end of the decade (see figure 1.2). At that point, the nonproliferation regime will be operationally bankrupt.

Today, North Korea has the unique distinction of being the world's only self-declared but unrecognized nuclear weapons state. U.S. intelligence analysts estimate that North Korea now has eight to ten weapons' worth of plutonium. This includes two weapons' worth that went missing before 1993; six bombs' worth that had been frozen at Yongbyong under the 1994 Agreed Framework and constantly inspected by the IAEA until 2003 when North Korea withdrew from the NPT;

Figure 1.2. Proliferation Hypotheticals, 2006–11

Timeline years: 2006, 2007, 2008, 2009, 2010, 2011

East Asian Scenario

2006: North Korea conducts nuclear weapons test; claims arsenal of 8–10 warheads.

2007: Japan withdraws from the Nuclear Non-Proliferation Treaty (NPT) despite heavy U.S. and Chinese pressure; announces robust nuclear deterrent within six months.

China accelerates nuclear deployments; Chinese-Japanese arms race begins.

2008: South Korea withdraws from the NPT and conducts nuclear test.

North Korea expands production of nuclear weapons from 3 to 12 a year.

2009: North Korea successfully tests Taepo-dong-3, a missile that can reliably carry nuclear warheads to the U.S. mainland; South Korea, fearing loss of U.S. deterrent, steps up nuclear-weapons production.

Growing arsenals of neighbcrs North Korea, Japan, a nd South Korea force adoption of hair-trigger launch protocols all around.

North Korean arsenal reaches sufficient size to allow covert sale of nuclear weapons; Venezuela and Nigeria are the first customers.

2010: Covert Taiwanese progress toward nuclear weapons capability leaked; China blockades Taiwan, demanding verifiable elimination of its nuclear program.

2011: Representatives of Al Qaeda and the North Korean government meet to discuss the purchase of multiple nuclear weapons.

Middle Eastern and South Asian Scenario

2007: Iran surprises world by conducting nuclear test; Middle East echoes with popular calls to counter the "Shia threat" and restore Sunni dignity by acquiring nuclear deterrent.

Iranian president Ahmadinejad reiterates former president Rafsanjani's threat that even a single nuclear weapon has the power to destroy Israel; Israel immediately acknowledges having at least 200 nuclear weapons and declares that any nuclear attack on it—including a terrorist attack—will result in the annihilation of Iran.

Oil prices spike sharply, "war risk" premium sustained indefinitely.

2008: Egypt launches crash nuclear program over stern Israeli and U.S. warnings; Syria initiates search for nuclear capabilities.

2009: Israel launches conventional preemptive strike against all known Egyptian nuclear facilities; war narrowly averted; wave of terror against Israel and United States begins.

2010: Saudi Arabia announces purchase of multiple nuclear weapons from an undisclosed seller (Pakistan is strongly suspected); threatens immediate use in face of any attack on it, conventional or otherwise.

United States, China, India, and others compete to export strategic oil reserves and lock up long-term contracts, pushing oil prices to new highs.

Source: The author's bad- (but not worst-) case scenario.

and two bombs' worth of material in spent fuel unloaded in February 2006.

In February 2006, North Korea declared itself a nuclear weapons state, claiming that it had "manufactured nukes for self-defense to cope with the Bush Administration's evermore undisguised policy to isolate and stifle the DPRK." Several months earlier, U.S. intelligence had sounded the alarm about what appeared to be North Korean preparations for a nuclear weapons test: construction of underground facilities and even a viewing stand near the northeast town of Kilju.

If North Korea tests a nuclear weapon and thus becomes, de facto, a recognized nuclear weapons state, what is likely to follow? Specifically, why should we anticipate the UN high level panel's feared cascade of proliferation?

Such a cascade is not inevitable. Currently the governments of Japan, South Korea, and Taiwan have reiterated their societies' long-standing commitment to reject nuclear weapons. The United States would surely make a maximum effort to reassure these governments and their citizens about the reliability of America's nuclear umbrella.

But if I had to bet, if North Korea conducts a test in 2006, forcing its recognition as a nuclear weapons state, within a decade Northeast Asia will include at least two more new nuclear states. In that scenario, the nuclear competition between Japan and China will likely escalate to resemble the Cold War competition between the United States and the Soviet Union.

Iran is testing the line in the Middle East. According to Tehran's narrative, Iran is exercising its "inalienable right" to build Iranian enrichment plants and make fuel for its peaceful civilian nuclear power generators. These same facilities, however, can continue enriching 3 or 4 percent U-235 to 90 percent U-235, which is the ideal core of a nuclear bomb. No one in the international community doubts that Iran's hidden objective in building enrichment facilities is to build nuclear bombs. If Iran crosses its nuclear finish line, a Middle Eastern cascade of new nuclear weapons states could trigger the first multiparty nuclear arms race, far more volatile than the Cold War competition between the United States and the Soviet Union.

Given Egypt's historic role as the leader of the Arab Middle East, the prospects of it living unarmed alongside a nuclear Persia are very low. The IAEA's reports of clandestine nuclear experiments hint that Cairo may have considered this possibility. Were Saudi Arabia to buy a dozen nuclear warheads that could be mated to the Chinese medium-range ballistic missiles it purchased secretly in the 1980s, few in the U.S. intelligence community would be surprised. Given Riyadh's role as the major financier of Pakistan's clandestine nuclear program in the 1980s, it is not out of the question that Riyadh and Islamabad have made secret arrangements for this contingency.

New Nuclear Dangers

Were a cascade of nuclear proliferation to occur in both the Middle East and Northeast Asia over the next decade, so what? How much should the Trilateral nations care? Five dimensions of danger provide grounds for serious concern:

1. Multiparty Mideast nuclear arms race. In 1962, bilateral competition between the United States and the Soviet Union led to the Cuban Missile Crisis, which historians now call "the most dangerous moment in human history." After the crisis, President Kennedy estimated the likelihood of nuclear war had been "between one in three and even." A multiparty nuclear arms race in the Middle East would be like playing Russian roulette with five bullets in a six-chamber revolver, dramatically increasing the likelihood of a regional nuclear war.

2. Accidental or unauthorized nuclear launch. A new nuclear weapons state goes through a period of nuclear adolescence that poses special dangers of accidental or unauthorized use—and Iran would be no different. When a state first acquires a small number of nuclear weapons, those weapons become a tempting target. Successful attack would disarm any capacity for a nuclear retaliation. Thus, fearing preemption, new nuclear weapons states rationally adopt loose command-and-control arrangements. But control arrangements loose enough to guard against decapitation inherently mean more fingers on more triggers and consequently more prospects of a nuclear weapons launch.

3. Theft from an uncertain Iranian regime. For outsiders, Iran appears to be a black box. Behind this exterior, however, are multiple centers of power and competing security structures. The supreme leader, Ayatollah Ali Khamenei, commands the armed forces and appears to have the last word on nuclear policy. But three other groups share constitutional authority over foreign policy with the supreme leader: President Mahmoud Ahmadinejad; former president Ali Akbar Hashemi Rafsanjani as head of the Expediency Council, which resolves conflicts among government branches; and the Foreign Ministry. Sharp differences among these groups reveal themselves in contradictory statements.

Could rogue elements within Iran's nuclear or security establishment divert nuclear weapons or nuclear materials to other nations or to terrorists? Considering that Iranian diplomats have offered to "transfer the experience, knowledge and technology of its scientists" to the genocide-tolerating government of Sudan, it is not difficult to imagine. Stop and think about the A. Q. Khan network, which sold designs, equipment, and materials to Libya, North Korea, Iran, and others. How hard would it be for an Iranian entrepreneur to follow in his footsteps?

4. An Israeli attack on Iran's nuclear facilities. Israel's military chief of staff has called an Iranian nuclear bomb "Israel's sole existential threat." Prime Minister Ehud Olmert has warned unambiguously, "Under no circumstances, and at no point, can Israel allow anyone with these kinds of malicious designs against us to have control of weapons of destruction that can threaten our existence."

The Israeli national security establishment has focused anxiously on a red line that Iran will cross when it achieves "technical independence" — sufficient knowledge about how to construct and operate a limited cascade of centrifuges that could produce enough HEU for an Iranian nuclear bomb. The head of Mossad, Israel's secret service, states publicly that Iran could cross that red line in 2006. In contrast, Washington talks about a different, and much later, red line: when Iran achieves industrial-level production of enriched uranium, or even operates a production facility long enough to produce a bomb's worth of material. U.S. intelligence continues to predict that this will take at least five years. It is possible, therefore, that Tel Aviv will make up its mind to strike Iran before the world has had time to fully consider its options.

Israel will not ask for U.S. permission before attacking Iranian nuclear facilities at Isfahan and Natanz. But the United States will be blamed throughout the Middle East as a hidden co-conspirator. Retaliation by the Iranian government and by those who sympathize with Osama bin Laden will target not only Israelis, but also Western interests, including oil-tanker traffic in the Persian Gulf.

5. North Korean nuclear bazaar. A nuclear-armed North Korea with a serial production line for an additional dozen weapons per year could become a nuclear Home Depot for rogue states and terrorist groups. Its top leadership has openly boasted that it intends to sell fissile material and even nuclear weapons—for the right price. During talks in Beijing in April 2003, North Korea's chief representative, Li Gun, told Assistant Secretary of State James Kelly that Pyongyang would "export nuclear weapons, add to its current arsenal, or test a nuclear device."

While missiles are North Korea's major crop, bringing in about $500 million annually, they are just one product in a catalog that includes illegal drugs and counterfeit currency. In essence, North Korea is a mafia state. Some of the regime's ambassadors fund their embassies through black-market dealings in methamphetamines, heroin, and cocaine. Japanese officials interdicted $335 million worth of North Korean methamphetamines in just one bust. In July 2002, Taiwanese police seized 175 pounds of heroin that had been smuggled through an official diplomatic channel. Throughout the 1990s, North Korean envoys working with European and Asian organized-crime groups were caught with thousands of counterfeit $100 bills in Mongolia, Russia, and Cambodia. This extensive experience in illicit international trade leaves North Korea supremely qualified to move fissile material around the globe to willing buyers. A case in point: despite close monitoring of North Korean exports by the Proliferation Security Initiative, last December Pyongyang successfully delivered to Iran 18 nuclear-capable BM-25 missiles with a 2,500-mile range.

After decades of relative calm, why are events that could tear apart the nonproliferation regime unfolding now? Obviously there are many reasons, stretching back at least two decades. Nonetheless, the single factor most responsible for the current nonproliferation regime crisis is the failure of the world's leading powers, first among them the self-identified "indispensable nation."

Fourteen years after the disappearance of the Soviet Union, we have much to applaud and for which to give thanks. Superpower nuclear arsenals left in three newly independent states of the former Soviet Union—Ukraine, Kazakhstan, and Belarus—were zeroed out of inventory. Those warheads were returned to Russia and dismantled. The HEU in them has been blended down and is being used today to produce half the electricity generated by nuclear power plants in the United States. Spurred and supported by the far-sighted U.S. Nunn-Lugar initiative, more than 22,000 tactical nuclear weapons and 4,000 strategic nuclear weapons were all returned to Russia from what became, overnight, 14 newly independent states. Most remarkable of all, despite the collapse of an empire and the chaos and corruption that ensued, not a single nuclear bomb from the former Soviet arsenal has yet been found outside Russia.

On the other hand, with their nuclear weapons tests in 1998, India and Pakistan have broken into the nuclear weapons club. Despite 80 percent reductions in their Cold War nuclear arsenals, both the United States and Russia have continued to emphasized the relevance—not the irrelevance—of nuclear weapons in international affairs.

For perspective on the historic opportunity missed over the past decade, it is instructive to compare the hope shared by the 173 nations participating in the Nuclear Nonproliferation Treaty Review Conference of 1995 with the despair that was the hallmark of the 2005 Review Conference last May.

In 1995, the countries that had voluntarily forsworn nuclear weapons by joining the NPT made their treaty commitment permanent by extending the treaty indefinitely. The nuclear powers were preparing to sign the Comprehensive Test Ban Treaty (CTBT) to eliminate all nuclear weapons trials. Prospects for concluding a fissile material cutoff by means of the Fissile Material Cut-off Treaty (FMCT) seemed excellent.

In contrast, the 2005 review conference was labeled by most participants a "bust." For this failure, there is more than enough blame for all parties. The United States insisted that the 13 commitments the nuclear weapons states had made as part of the 2000 review conference were "no longer operational," that the word "disarmament" could not appear in any communiqué by the conference, and that U.S. discussions about the need for additional new nuclear weapons did not conflict with their treaty commitment to diminish the role of nuclear weapons in international affairs. The nonnuclear weapons states refused to address the treaty's nonproliferation loopholes if disarmament was not on the table, and the ensuing uproar prevented the conference from tackling the urgent challenge posed to the entire nonproliferation system by North Korea and Iran.

A Strategy for Prevention

The largely unrecognized good news is that nuclear terrorism is, in fact, preventable—preventable by a feasible, affordable checklist of actions. A strategy for pursuing that agenda can be organized under the Doctrine of Three No's: no loose nukes, no new nascent nukes, and no new nuclear weapons states.[6] The strategic narrows in this challenge are to prevent terrorists from acquiring nuclear weapons or the materials from which weapons could be made. If this choke point can be squeezed tightly enough, we can deny terrorists the means necessary for the most deadly of all terror acts. As a fact of physics—no highly enriched uranium or plutonium, no nuclear explosion, no nuclear terrorism—it is that simple.

No Loose Nukes

No loose nukes requires securing all nuclear weapons and weapons-usable material, on the fastest possible timetable, to a new "gold standard." Locking up valuable or dangerous items is something we know how to do. The United States does not lose gold from Fort Knox, nor does Russia lose treasures from the Kremlin armory. Washington and Moscow should jointly develop a standard and then act at once to secure their own nuclear materials. President Vladimir Putin must come to feel this existential threat to Russia in his gut. Moscow must see safeguarding those weapons not as a favor to the United States but as an essential protection for its own country and citizens.

With Putin aboard, the United States and Russia should launch a new global alliance against nuclear terrorism. Its mission would be to lock down all weapons and materials everywhere and clean out what cannot be locked down. This would require engaging the leaders of other nuclear states on the basis of a bedrock of vital national interest: preventing a nuclear bomb from going off in my capital. The global cleanout of at-risk nuclear material must be accelerated to finish the job in the next 12 to 18 months.

No New Nascent Nukes

No new nascent nukes means no new national capabilities to enrich uranium or reprocess plutonium. A loophole in the 1968 NPT allows states to develop these capacities as civilian programs, withdraw from the treaty, utilize equipment and know-how received as a beneficiary of the treaty, and proceed to build nuclear weapons. The proposition of no new nascent nukes acknowledges what the national security community has been slow in realizing: HEU and plutonium are bombs just about to hatch.

---

6 Allison, *Nuclear Terrorism*, part 2.

The crucial challenge to this principle today is Iran. Preventing Iranian completion of its nuclear infrastructure will require a combination of enticing incentives and credible threats to persuade Tehran to accept a grand bargain for denuclearization. The United States should engage Iran in direct negotiations in coordination with a six-party complement that includes the EU-3 and Russia. The United States threatens what Iran's leadership worries about most, namely, regime change— President Bush's announced goal in his declaration of the "axis of evil." Despite U.S. difficulties in reconstructing a post-Saddam Iraq, Iran's leaders took note of U.S. military capabilities that destroyed in a mere two weeks their most hated and feared adversary. President Bush should be prepared to give Tehran a security assurance that the United States will not use force to attack Iran to change its regime as long as Iran complies with the terms of a moratorium on nuclear enrichment activity and permits intrusive IAEA inspections. To assure that the moratorium is observed not only at Isfahan and Natanz but everywhere in Iran, these inspections must exceed the Additional Protocol, which allows inspections on short notice of suspected nuclear sites but does not allow access to military facilities or officials.

The partners should bring to these negotiations all the carrots the international community can reasonably provide Iran. These include a formal Iranian-EU agreement for significantly increased trade and investments; the opportunity to purchase additional civilian nuclear reactors from Russia (Iranian plans call for 10 over the next decade); assured supply of fuel for nuclear reactors from internationally supervised suppliers—to include Russia, the EU, the United States, and a special IAEA-controlled "reserve of last resort" against the extreme contingency that the supply of fuel could to be interrupted for noncommercial reasons—as proposed by IAEA director Mohamed ElBaradei; spare parts from the United States for Iran's aging aircraft; an opportunity to buy new Airbus aircraft from Europe; the beginning of negotiations with the World Trade Organization about membership; and a commitment to six-party talks about Iran's larger security concerns and those of the region. This package could also include an offer by the United States to open its embassy in Tehran, to allow the Islamic Republic to open an embassy in Washington, and to begin discussion about normalization of relations.

Carrots alone will not suffice. Crucial to sealing this deal will be a judgment by Iran's leaders that they have no realistic prospect of enriching uranium on an industrial scale. Essential to that judgment is a credible military threat to destroy the facilities before they can become operational. Since the point is the threat, not the act, central casting has provided an ideal threatener. Prime Minister Ehud Olmert has committed Israel to "making sure no one has the capability or the power to commit destruction against us." In light of the assertion by Iranian president Mahmoud Ahmadinejad that "Israel must be wiped off the map," Israeli preemptive action should not be difficult for Iran to imagine.

What remains for this deal to come together is for the United States to step up as a determined deal maker, assemble the full array of international carrots, and package a deal Iran cannot reasonably refuse.

No New Nuclear Weapons States

No new nuclear weapons states draws a bright line under the current eight nuclear powers and says unambiguously: "No more." The urgent test of this principle is North Korea, which now stands halfway across that line. Preventing Pyongyang from becoming a Nukes "R" Us for terrorists is the biggest challenge the international community faces in the Asian arena.

The best hope for resolution starts with the joint declaration at last September's six-party talks in which North Korea committed itself to "abandon all nuclear weapons and existing programs and return, at an early date, to the Treaty on the Nonproliferation of Nuclear Weapons and to IAEA safeguards." Between those words and the realization of this objective lies a long, steep road—every step of which will be complex and contested. The first step must be a North Korean freeze of its Yongbyon reactor and the associated reprocessing facility that is producing an additional two bombs' worth of plutonium annually. Persuading Kim Jong-Il to take even this step has so far proved impossible for the other members of the six-party talks.

Between North Korea and Washington there is zero trust. Each believes it was cheated by the other in prior agreements, and the evidence supports both parties' claims. Given this deep distrust, China is the state best situated to play a critical role. When China earlier interrupted the flow of oil to Pyongyang "for technical reasons," North Korea's response was swift and compliant. China will thus have to be a central actor in the design of a ministep-by-ministep process in which the other five members of the six-party talks provide benefits to North Korea for the freeze and ultimate dismantling of its nuclear weapons infrastructure.

From the outset, the six-party talks have been stalemated by the fact that the stated U.S. objective—collapse of the North Korean regime—is China's worst nightmare. In China's dominant narrative, it entered the Korean War to prevent a U.S.-allied government on its border with Korea. As a concession to China, the Bush administration should subordinate North Korean regime change to stopping North Korea's nuclear program. This should include an assurance that the United States will not station troops in North Korea in any circumstance. President Bush should pledge this immediately. The United States must demonstrate readiness to join in multinational, Chinese-led assurances that North Korea will not be attacked as long as it observes constraints on further production or export of nuclear materials and begins small steps toward eliminating its nuclear arsenal.

With these carrots from the United States, with South Korean willingness to deepen economic relations in an evolutionary process to reunify the Korean peninsula, and with economic and technical assistance offered by Japan and China, China should be able to persuade North Korea's Kim Jong-Il to freeze current nuclear activities.

In addition, the responsible members of the international community should articulate credibly a principle of nuclear accountability. States should be held accountable for nuclear weapons and nuclear material they produce. North Korea should be put on notice that any nuclear attack using a weapon or weapon built from fissile material that originated within its borders will be treated as an attack by North Korea and will be met with "a full retaliatory response."

The world has made significant strides on this agenda since the 9/11 wake-up call to the threat of megaterrorism. The United Nations Security Council successfully passed Resolution 1540, requiring all states to criminalize proliferation, and the UN General Assembly adopted the International Convention for the Suppression of Acts of Nuclear Terrorism that encourages information sharing to prevent and prosecute acts of nuclear terrorism. The Proliferation Security Initiative—which permits the search of any vehicle suspected of transporting WMD cargo—now includes more than 60 participating nations. At the 2002 meeting of the G-8, members committed to match America's $1 billion annual contribution over the next decade to secure and eliminate former Soviet nuclear weapons. Nine potential nuclear weapons have been removed from Yugoslavia, Romania, Bulgaria, Uzbekistan, the Czech Republic, and Kazakhstan. The new U.S.-led Global Threat Reduction Initiative has removed bomb-making materials from risky research reactors around the world. Libyan leader Muammar Qadhafi renounced his nuclear weapons program, and the secret black-market network of Pakistani scientist A. Q. Khan was exposed.

And yet, for all the international activity on this agenda, what has been the net result as of April 2006?

The Global Report Card for Preventing Nuclear Terrorism:

Subject	Since 9/11	Overall grade
No loose nukes	↑	B–
No new nascent nukes	↓	C–
No new nuclear weapons states	↓	F

An Agenda for Stopping Proliferation and Preventing Nuclear Terrorism Now

The leaders of the world who meet in St. Petersburg in July 2006 for the G-8 summit have a great opportunity to avert both the collapse of the nonproliferation regime and a sharp increase in the likelihood of nuclear terrorism. Their agenda should include four urgent undertakings:

1. Make the prevention of nuclear terrorism and the further spread of nuclear weapons an absolute priority. One small nuclear bomb in New York or Moscow or Tokyo would be a world-altering event. For perspective, consider that Al Qaeda's September 11, 2001, attack took 2,986 souls. A crude nuclear device detonated in lower Manhattan would kill half a million people and cause more than $1 trillion of damage. Researchers at RAND, a U.S. government-funded think tank, have estimated that a nuclear explosion would cause indirect costs worldwide of more than $3 trillion, shutting down U.S. ports and cutting world trade by $730 billion. The gravity of these consequences requires that absolute priority be given to the challenge of stopping nuclear terrorism. In the Cold War, we recognized that preventing a global nuclear war was a necessary condition for pursuing any other objective. Ronald Reagan stated, in his oft-quoted one-liner: "A nuclear war can never be won and must never be fought." The categorical imperative therefore is to do everything technically feasible on the fastest possible timeline to prevent it. As the Japanese Peace Memorial Museum of Hiroshima memorializes poignantly in stone, "To remember Hiroshima is to abhor nuclear war."

2. Establish a global alliance against nuclear terrorism. The United States cannot undertake or sustain the war on nuclear terrorism alone. Nor can the necessary actions simply be commanded, compelled, or coerced. Instead they require deep and steady international cooperation rooted in a recognition that the civilized states share an overriding common threat and can succeed only with a common strategy.

Each nation's best hope for achieving conditions essential for its own security requires serious cooperation with the others. The great powers are therefore ripe for the mobilization of a new grand alliance against nuclear terrorism. The mission of this alliance should be to minimize the risk of nuclear terrorism by taking every action physically, technically, and diplomatically possible to prevent nuclear weapons or materials from falling into the hands of terrorists.

Existing alliances are ill-suited to address this global security threat. NATO covers one regional area, the U.S.–Japanese Security Treaty another. The nuclear nonproliferation "regime" consists of a patchwork of treaties like the NPT; informal agreements like the Nuclear Suppliers Group and the Proliferation Security Initiative; nuclear-free zones in Latin America, Southeast Asia, and the Australia-Pacific region; and assorted bilateral agreements. Meeting the global threat of nuclear terrorism will require a comprehensive global response.

Construction of this new alliance should begin with the United States and Russia. Americans and Russians have a special obligation to address this problem because they created it—and because they still own 95 percent of all nuclear weapons and materials. More than a decade of cooperation in the Nunn-Lugar Cooperative Threat Reduction Program, the G-8 global partnership, and most recently the commitments of President Bush and President Putin at the Bratislava summit of February 2005 provide a foundation from which to step up to the next level. Initially, members of the alliance would join in five common undertakings.

First, they would embrace a principle of assured nuclear security to guarantee that all nuclear weapons and materials on their own territory are secured to a "gold standard"—beyond the reach of terrorists or thieves. The leader of each country would pledge to the other leaders to personally hold accountable the entire government chain of command to quickly achieve this result. Understanding that each country bears the responsibility for the security of its own nuclear materials, the members should nonetheless offer any technical and financial assistance required to make this happen. Assured nuclear security requires sufficient transparency to allow other leaders to reassure their own citizens that terrorists will never get a nuclear bomb from another member of this alliance.

Second, the alliance would shape a global consensus in support of enforcing the three no's, beginning with North Korea, Iran, and Pakistan. During the Cold War, when the United States and the Soviet Union cooperated, nuclear aspirants were stymied. Only when one of the nuclear powers cooperated with a nuclear hopeful, or during periods when the superpowers were competing or distracted, did new nuclear weapons states realize their ambitions. India and Pakistan offer vivid examples. The failure of the United States and Russia to hold back these two nations led to India and Pakistan testing weapons openly and declaring themselves nuclear weapons states in 1998. Subsequent Russian–U.S.–Chinese cooperation in nudging India and Pakistan back from the nuclear brink suggests what can be accomplished by concerted effort.

Third, the new alliance should reinvent a more robust nonproliferation regime to control the sale and export of nuclear technologies, materials, and know-how. The frightening facts about A. Q. Khan's global black market should inspire comparably determined counteractions to head off similar networks. Criminalization of all proliferation activities, required by UN Security Council Resolution 1540, is a step in this direction. The resolution, adopted April 28, 2004, calls for securing nuclear weapons, materials, and technologies by requiring all states to pass laws outlawing proliferation, to enact strict export controls, and to secure sensitive materials within their borders. Although the resolution obligates sovereign states to close the loopholes exploited by black-market WMD networks, it currently lacks necessary enforcement mechanisms.

Fourth, the new alliance should adapt lessons learned from U.S.–Russian, U.S.–Chinese, and other cooperative ventures to the campaign against the Taliban and Al Qaeda. These include the importance of intelligence sharing and affirmative counterproliferation. While the new *International Convention for the Suppression of Acts of Nuclear Terrorism* encourages states to share information about nuclear proliferation and trafficking, the alliance would provide a formal infrastructure. In addition to intelligence sharing, joint training for preemption against terrorists, criminal groups, or rogue states attempting to acquire WMD would provide an enforcement mechanism for alliance commitments.

Finally, this alliance should be not just a signed document but a living institution committed to its mission. Like the G-8, the leaders of key member states should meet annually; their ministers, quarterly. But, unlike the G-8 and more like NATO, the alliance should have a secretariat that coordinates working groups on specific topics, develops work plans, and tracks performance in meeting milestones. In the process, the members should develop shared assessments of threats and identify actions member states can take, individually and collectively, to address the dangers. Moreover, they should identify activities beyond the agenda that advance the mission of the alliance, including topics that will be uncomfortable for some members, such as the CTBT or the appropriateness of new programs in the established nuclear states.

3. A fourth no? Objections will surely be raised about the unfairness of a regime in which some states are allowed to possess nuclear weapons while others are not. But that distinction is already embedded in the NPT, to which all nonnuclear weapons states except North Korea are signatories. Although the treaty nominally commits nuclear weapons states to eventually eliminate their own weapons, it sets no timetable, and was not expected to happen soon.

The leading nuclear states have the power to define and enforce global constraints on nuclear weapons. By doing so they can preserve all nations from the nightmare of nuclear terrorists destroying civilization as we know it. To make this order acceptable, these nations must work harder to marginalize the role of nuclear weapons and nuclear threats in international affairs. This requires no new nukes by nuclear weapons states (contrary to the Bush administration's current efforts), no nuclear tests (and thus the ratification of the CTBT, which the Bush administration has refused to consider), no new production of fissile material leading to early ratification of the FMCT (which the recent U.S.-India nuclear agreement risks compromising), and no brandishing of nuclear threats (contrary to President Jacques Chirac's recent outburst or the Pentagon's reported examination of nuclear strikes against Iran).

4. Bolster the NPT by establishing an assured nuclear fuel supply. For peaceful nuclear power to prosper, dangerous nuclear materials must be secured. Given the growth of global demand for energy to fuel current and future economic growth, civilian nuclear power plants should become a larger source of supply. Presidents Bush and Putin have each proposed programs to make nuclear energy accessible to countries that want it, without spreading the infrastructure for nuclear weapons.

The NPT bargain promises states that pledge not to acquire nuclear weapons "the benefits of peaceful application of nuclear technology." The promise of peaceful nuclear energy, however, is hostage to the safety and security of dangerous atoms. States must be able to buy and build nuclear power plants with reliable assurances of nuclear fuel and its disposal (including the plutonium encased within it). Director General Mohamed ElBaradei of the IAEA has proposed such a system: a nuclear fuel reserve that would assure to states that forgo enrichment and reprocessing a guaranteed supply of fuel at bargain prices from multiple internationally supervised suppliers including the United States, Russia, and a European consortium. An IAEA-controlled reserve would serve as a backstop against nuclear fuel interruption for noncommercial reasons.

Conclusion

The twentieth century's leading business thinker, Peter Drucker, died in 2005 at age 95. Drucker frequently warned, "Plans are only good intentions unless they immediately degenerate into hard work."

The painful truth is that failure to prevent the spread of nuclear weapons and the use of such weapons by terrorists would result from a failure of will, not of words or of means. Having enjoyed six decades without the use of nuclear weapons as a result of the strenuous, steady actions of courageous leaders, this generation of leaders must ask what excuse it will give its successors if it bequeaths them a world of nuclear anarchy.

2

Iran Case Study:
Is There a "Plan B" for Iran?

Hervé de Carmoy

The decision by the International Atomic Energy Agency (IAEA) in March 2006 to refer Iran and its nuclear program to the United Nations Security Council sparked a nasty exchange of threats. Iranian officials said Iran would bring "harm and pain" to its critics, especially the United States, if punishments were meted out to it. U.S. officials responded by labeling Iran and its apparent nuclear ambitions as the country's biggest current challenge. For the moment, the great powers—the United States, France, Germany, Britain, Russia, India, and China—seem unified in the view that all options except referral to the Security Council have been exhausted.

Beyond that, however, agreement may be far harder to reach on appropriate forms of punitive action.

What might be the way forward? Three questions need to be answered in order to explore the possible scenarios:

- Is the prospect of a regime change in Iran plausible?
- Is a preemptive military strike a viable option?
- Can diplomacy and creative compromise be an alternative?

Is the Prospect of a Regime Change in Iran Plausible?

Some think Iran is such an enigma that this question is unanswerable. The reply from a European point of view is hardly straightforward:

The author wishes to acknowledge the support provided by Ambassador Lubrani of the Office of the Prime Minister of Israel; Bill Emmott, former editor in chief of the *Economist*; and Terence Ward, a leading expert on Iran.

- Iran is a country of 68 million people that had only 35 million people 25 years ago.

- Iran has a gross domestic product (GDP) of $182 billion, $40 billion in hard currency, proven oil reserves of 133 billion barrels, and a yearly oil production of 4 billion barrels.

- In Iran, 40 percent of the people live below the poverty line, and the country has 2 million drug users.

- The Islamic regime has established numerous new universities. Current university enrollment is estimated at 1 million students. In this situation, approximately 1 million university graduates join the labor market every four years, most of them remaining unemployed. Iran's official unemployment rate currently stands at 15-17 percent, with most of the unemployed being university graduates. Their actual number is significantly higher than that indicated by official sources.

- The inflation rate in Iran is rising and has officially reached 18 percent a year (the real percentage is much higher). This situation has not been alleviated by the regime, which does not redistribute the immense profits it has made, thanks to the rise in oil prices, in order to prevent an additional increase in inflation.

- According to a World Bank report, 60 percent of Iranians between the ages of 30 and 49 live in poverty, and more than 1.3 million people earn less than $1 a day.

- The change of generations has led to a significant increase in the number of senior officers retiring from long military service (primarily in the Revolutionary Guards), who are now striving for places in the regime. This is exacerbated by the rift within the reformist bloc, which is still a part of the regime. This rift was best seen in the regime's inability to offer an agreed-upon candidate for the presidential elections (June 17, 2005) as well as through the reformists' failure to present an agreed-upon candidate of their own.

- Each year, some 150,000 to 200,000 citizens leave Iran, most of them possessing the best education available, and if Iran's doors were truly to open we would be witnessing a major exodus of people. This phenomenon, stemming from internal pressures on one hand and the influence of the Iranian diaspora on the other, is a permanent and dominant factor that is shaping Iranian society.

- The restlessness among the ethnic groups composing Iranian society has grown stronger, even though there is no coordination among these groups and no indication of an organized movement. Nevertheless, the Arabs in Khuzestan, the Iranian Kurds, the Baloch, the Khorasanis, and others are affected by regional events such as Iraq, Afghanistan, Kiev, and Lebanon.

In brief, Iran presents most of the characteristics of a developing country endowed with considerable oil resources. But there is more to Iran than oil and misdirected riches. The Iranians' national psyche is deeply historic and nationalistic. The survival of the Persian language and Persian art testifies to the robustness of this civilization and to Iranians' demand for recognition of their strategic centrality.

Another facet of Iranian identity is Shia particularism. Today Iran remains the only nation with this proclaimed faith enshrined in its constitution. The political manipulation of this Shia branch of Islam has resulted in an ideology based on ostensible dogmatic religious principles that provides draconian legal justification for suppressing human rights. This is manifested in the discrimination toward the non-Farsi and religious minorities (Bahais, Armenian Christians, Jews, and Zoroastrians) and in the regime's ostracism toward Israel and the Jews.

In fact, violations of human rights, imprisonment and torture, mass executions, arrests of Iranian journalists and intellectuals, and bans and excommunications in the name of religion have all increased since the Islamic Revolution in 1979.

At the same time, Tehran has become the center of radical militant Islam and the focus of support and direction for Islamist terrorism around the globe. Iran is currently involved in a proxy war between Sunni and Shia in Iraq, disrupting coalition efforts to create a stable democracy there. Some do not believe that Iran is actually trying to incite civil war in Iraq because this would destroy the chances of Iraq's elected central government that will be led and dominated by Shia when it is eventually formed, although the threat of civil war may be what is meant by "harm and pain" to the United States. Iran is involved in efforts to derail any hope of an Israeli-Palestinian settlement, in fomenting belligerency in the Persian Gulf, and, last but not least, in incessant efforts to achieve nuclear weapons. The blatant disregard by the Islamic regime of basic human rights and civil liberties stands in contradiction with the goal of a "greater Middle East" founded on democratic values and promoted by the United States.

The election of Tehran's mayor, 48-year-old Mahmoud Ahmadi-nejad—an unknown personality at the time both inside and outside Iran—as Iran's new president is turning out to be a choice made expressly to address the political, economic, and military challenges posed to Iran and its regime by the new U.S.-led situation in the Middle East. There is now no doubt that his landslide victory over one of Iran's most powerful leaders, Hashemi Rafsanjani, was an engineered result of advance planning, organization, and exceptional efforts on the part of key figures of the Iranian regime's leadership.

Ahmadinejad ran on a populist platform pledging to redistribute oil wealth to the poor, remove the elite who dominate the oil industry, and provide a better economic future for long-suffering Iranians. He tapped into the vein of popular anger against corruption and cronyism by promising jobs to unemployed youth, better salaries to underpaid workers, as well as food and housing for the poor.

His opponent, Hashemi Rafsanjani, suffered from recent accusations—by the imprisoned journalist Akbar Ganji—that he profited handsomely as president from commissions on military purchases during the long and bloody Iraq-Iran War. Rumored to be the wealthiest man in Iran, Rafsanjani was unelectable. Ahmadinejad's radical promises jeopardized the vested interests of the Iranian business class whom Rafsanjani represents. Although Rafsanjani lost dramatically, he remains a crucial power broker and head of the Expediency Council, which now has oversight over the president.

What happened in Tehran was, in fact, an important regime change brought about by so-called democratic means: it has become more Islamist, more Khomeinist, more militant, and more nationalist. This new government brought to power the second generation of Islamic revolutionaries, the commanders of the Revolutionary Guards who, by and large, subscribe to radical, militant policies in all that concerns Iran's internal as well as foreign affairs. They may well represent the last, desperate act by hard-line extremists to evoke once again a revolutionary resurgence in a society that has moved far beyond the tired slogans of the past and is considered by most analysts to be the most pro-Western society in the Middle East. Nevertheless, the president and his allies consider themselves committed to follow to the letter Ayatollah Ruhollah Khomeini's teachings:

- Aspiration for leadership over the Islamic world and an unconditional return to radical fundamentalist Islam;

- Hatred of the West and its culture, led by the United States as the symbol of evil—the Great Satan; and

- Denial of Israel's existence and a constant striving to harm it in any way possible, perceiving it as the symbol and spearhead of the West in general and the United States in particular.

There is little question that Ahmadinejad hopes to take on the mantle of Khomeini. In the 1970s Khomeini declared that the shah's illegal regime must disappear, and it happened. He also said that the Soviet Union would disappear, and it happened. He even said that the evil Saddam Hussein must be punished, and there Saddam is, standing trial in his own country. Khomeini added, "The occupying regime of Al-Quds (Jerusalem) must be wiped off the map of the world, and with God's help we will soon witness a world without America and Zionism, despite those who doubt it."

Above and beyond oil, nationalism, and Islamic fervor, some additional dimensions are necessary to understand the dynamics at work in Iran.

Demographic Facts

With 30 million Iranians below the age of 30, there is a huge latent human power base that can be mobilized in opposite directions. It can become the fertile ground for popular unrest and political instability.

Iran has one of the most youthful and educated populations in the Middle East. The literacy rate in the generation under 30 is well over 90 percent. In 2005, more than 65 percent of those entering university were women. Those who have lived throughout the Iranian revolution of 1979 are now a minority. Few doubt that it is this younger generation that will ultimately determine the future of Iran.

As the gap between the rulers and the ruled widens, extremists have raised the volume on their hard-line rhetoric, trying to reassert Iran's radical credentials. Yet, according to surveys by Iran's own Ministry of Culture and Guidance, less than 1.4 percent of the population attends Friday prayers.

But effective subversion requires massive soft skills, time, and money. So far, exiles do not appear to be having much impact persuading young and nationalist Iranians, most of whom are proud of the nuclear program. In fact, the vast majority of Iranians of all political persuasions—from the archconservative right to liberal democrats on the left—maintain adamantly that Iran's nuclear program is a national right, a question of honor, a sign of progress, and a symbol of scientific achievement. Even with regime change, it should be expected that a democratic regime would assume the same position.

The skill sets and commitment of a modern version of Radio Free Europe are not yet available. The bridge to the young people has not been built up. Resentment against dire economic circumstances has not been transformed into rebellion. Brutal crackdowns that crushed the student movement and popular demonstrations over the past decade have ingrained a profound fear of violent reprisals. This fear has kept disaffected Iranians off the streets.

So far the leadership of Iran has seized on the one strategy that touches a sensitive chord among millions of Iranians. Iran is in search of regional preeminence not unlike that of France at the turn of the nineteenth century and of Germany later on. Such a dream can mobilize youth in Iran. It can create the psychological and political environment that would make possible an attempt to neutralize the Supreme Leader Ali Khamenei and replace him with a man close to his own convictions. Khamenei has been startled by Ahmadinejad's disruptive tendencies, yet he has reacted and granted oversight over the presidency to the Expediency Council (the nonelected body headed by Rafsanjani). In fact, the current president has less legal power than any of his Islamic Republic predecessors.

Political and Diplomatic Skills of the Regime

Let there be no doubt where power rests today. It lies in clerical rule: the supreme leader, the president, the Guardian Council, the Islamic Revolutionary Guard, the Expediency Council, and the recently strengthened police forces (Law Enforcement Forces). These structures counterbalance the Parliament and the regular army. They provide great strength to the elites who have allocated considerable resources to finance them and thus to shore up their power base. The police and paramilitary forces are often garrisoned near populated areas and dispersed throughout the country. They will be difficult to confront in a way that would loosen the regime's grip on power.

In addition, the regime leaders are shrewd observers of the tectonic changes in the world geopolitical relationships. Having lived for decades with a siege mentality, they are determined to seize what they perceive to be an historic opportunity for Iran, all the more as Iranian firsthand knowledge of the United States is most limited.

These leaders feel they can exploit to their regional advantage the rise of China and India with their interests in competition with those of the United States, the nuclear and military technology and greed of Russia, the declining legitimacy of the United States, and the very soft power indeed of the European Union.

Russia and China in particular are perceived as ad hoc strategic allies for procurement of military and nuclear technology, for oil exports, gasoline and other imports, and for political support against any potential U.S. intervention. Together with India, Russia and China are now primary, not secondary, players in the Iran standoff. The announcement in 2005 of the flight of $50 billion in Iranian foreign assets from European banks signals a strategic move to eliminate Europe's critical leverage.

Finally, the Hamas gains in Palestine and, more important, the Shia success in Iraq are sweet victories for Iran's theocrats. The latter point is the most fundamental. The Shia in Iraq have become the objective ally of the United States in Iraq. It is the Sunni insurgents who are killing U.S. troops. It is the Sunni, with fundamentalist Saudi financing, who are refusing to accept the new reality. To put it in simple terms, U.S. interests in securing and pacifying Iraq are now squarely in the hands of Shia leadership. Iraqi Shia leaders will never accept or support a U.S. attack on Iran. These are major trump cards in Iran's future negotiations with the United States, together with the Iranian leadership's knowledge that the global weapon is energy.

In reality, Iran may increasingly look east to China as its future success model. Single-party political control, coupled with an expanding, prosperous economy and a strong military capability, may be its only hope of survival. Indeed, Iran may feel protected by its Asian and Russian economic partners because of its conviction that they will veto at the UN Security Council any proposal for military action.

But the West still holds major trump cards. It represents 75 percent of global wealth and 95 percent of world military power. Democracy is gaining some initial momentum in most of the Middle East, from Lebanon to Jordan, from the United Arab Emirates to Saudi Arabia.

The West should be alert to, but not yet taken in by, the theatrics of the present regime. Iran is not irrational and can be deterred. Several generations of leaders since Khomeini in 1987 have had the supremacy of state interests at the top of their agenda ahead of revolutionary doctrine and religious purity. Decision makers have sought to minimize risks. They have shunned direct confrontation. They still provide the IAEA with the minimum information required to keep the process alive. They use surrogates such as the Lebanese Hezbollah for violent actions. They are keen observers of what it takes to survive.

The appeal and the impact of Ahmadinejad's declarations and diatribes must be put into context—unless he topples Supreme Leader Khamenei. Ahmadinejad is constrained by the fact that his minority Shia sect has been considered heretical by 90 percent of the Muslims in the world since the seventh century, by their use of the Persian language, and by Iranian ethnicity. For instance, there are violent Sunni groups in Pakistan that have declared Shia non-Muslims. Al Qaeda leaders have called for war against the Shia in Iraq, and the Muslim Brotherhood in Egypt rejects Shia beliefs. Both forms of political Sunni Islam—Al Qaeda and the Brotherhood—have common ideological origins. Both have their roots in antisecular opposition in Egypt, a conservative reading of Sunni Islam, and the wealth and religious zeal of the Saudis. For the Saudi Wahhabis—eager funders of most expressions of contemporary militant Sunni Islam from Indonesia, Malaysia, Pakistan, Iraq, Palestine, Egypt, Bosnia, Chechnya, and Europe—the greatest threat on the horizon is not the West but rather Shia Iran and now Shia Iraq.

All of this is understood and perceived, inside and outside Iran, and may markedly reduce any threat of Ahmadinejad's emergence as a populist Islamic leader. We should not underestimate the true scope of the religious struggle within Islam and the relative weakness of Iran's brand of Islam, all the more so as Najaf in Iraq is fighting the city of Qom to regain its primary role within the Shia community.

Finally, the West has not yet begun to mobilize its resources in a coherent and integrated way to neutralize this twenty-first-century form of an old European disease: fascism in Islamic clothing.

Nonmilitary options for Europe and the United States could include demonstrating seriousness by taking the Mujahedin-e Khalq off the list of terrorist organizations and by seeking systematic actions that hurt the regime, from labor unrest in the oil industry to sharp reductions in the export to Iran of finished oil products. Iran imports 145,000 barrels per day (b/d) of gasoline from Kuwait, Saudi Arabia, and Abu Dhabi. Gasoline consumption is soaring in Iran. It is forecast to rise to 400,000 b/d with domestic refineries being able to produce only 245,000 b/d. If the export of oil products to Iran were to be partially or totally blocked with the support of India, which has a gasoline surplus, the internal impact on Iran could be massive.

In conclusion, the likelihood of a regime change in Iran induced by an internal opposition receiving support from outside is distant. But there is no reason for the West not to work intelligently to weaken the grip on power of the present theocrats. Reaching out to pragmatists through back channels is an important strategy to consider. Many pragmatists are in conflict and disagree with the direction that the current radicals are taking. Ahmadinejad is increasingly viewed as an extremist loose cannon. The three losers in the controversial presidential election are noteworthy figures — Mehdi Karroubi (onetime speaker of Parliament), Mostafa Moin (former education minister), and Hashemi Rafsanjani (former president); each represents factional power blocs within Iran and has continued to mock Ahmadinejad. The internal rivalry between the Right and the extreme Right now offers an opportunity for reformists to regroup. Many pragmatists in the Iranian power structure do not agree with the radical faction's attempt to isolate Iran internationally for its own ends. They may be willing to back down on the nuclear issue to save the economy, their own careers, and the Islamic Republic.

What is needed is a transatlantic commitment exercised in a discreet and integrated manner, while recognizing that the ultimate solution must also deal with Iran's security problem. There is justification for Iran to feel surrounded by potential enemies — Pakistan, Iraq, Russia, the United States — and hence to build new ties, notably with China and India. But should China, India, and Russia prove to be moderately supportive of the U.S.-UN approach, the West still has significant trump cards to play.

Is a Preemptive Military Strike a Viable Option?

The military option raises issues at several levels: geopolitical, moral, and tactical.

Issues of Geopolitics

All parties concerned are confronted with a high-risk situation, definite rewards, and a complex set of circumstances, many of which are unpredictable. Why? Because Iran is today at the center of an interdependent world; developments and geopolitical choices of the major actors have an impact on all of the others. This is why their relative strengths, motivations, and red lines need analysis in order to better understand the framework within which military action can take place.

Iran. Iran's primary national interests lie in the Persian Gulf (Iran's *mare nostrum*). Above and beyond security, these include maritime export routes for oil, demands on the Gulf states for territory, and reduced oil quotas to obtain higher prices for Iranian oil. Iran's key strategic goal today is to raise the ante for U.S. involvement in the region through the use of religious incitement, military threats, and terrorism. Islamic Jihad and Hezbollah are receiving money and weapons valued in the high eight figures from Iran. The threat to Israel of the rocket infrastructure located in South Lebanon and manned with the help of the Iranian Revolutionary Guards and the support of Syria is real. A nuclear Iran may be a watershed for the balance of power between Iran and its neighbors, and it could coerce some of them into accepting actions detrimental to them or to their neighbors. As Iran gets closer to a military nuclear capability with long-range delivery systems, a nonconventional arms race with its neighbors becomes more likely. This concerns Egypt; also, Saudi Arabia may ask for Pakistani assistance.

Let us also remember that when France sold military equipment to Qatar, Bahrain, and the United Arab Emirates, these countries were provided as part of the sale with security guarantees. The United Kingdom did the same with Oman. These countries may soon start calling in those promises.

Finally there is the possibility that a nuclear Iran might provide nuclear material to terrorist organizations or to other so-called states of concern.

Europe. The European initiative of 2003 had benefits and shortcomings. It allowed all parties concerned to gain a much clearer understanding of Iranian nuclear activities. The radical declarations of President Ahmadinejad to no small extent helped build a multilateral consensus against Iran. Time may have been gained, however; but the Iranian challenge has not yet been confronted. Two assumptions have been proved unfounded: The rate of democratic reform in Iran has not preceded the maturation of its military nuclear program, and, furthermore, engagement has not mitigated Iran's radicalism and strengthened the reformist camp. The question remains whether a window of opportunity will remain open for the United States and Europe with enough time for constructive diplomacy. It might if the United States and Europe continue to develop an integrated approach with high-urgency lines of communication and cooperation to China, India, Japan, and Russia—which are major customers, suppliers, neighbors, and military powers and can influence Iran. A predominantly U.S.-Eurocentric diplomatic approach is unlikely to succeed.

Russia. Russia is in transition, as highlighted by the recently published Trilateral task force report, *Engaging with Russia: the Next Phase,* by Sir Roderic Lyne, Strobe Talbott and Koji Watanabe.[1]

The question remains whether there is room for a partnership with Russia on Iran. The answer could be positive if it is constructed in a way perceived by Russia to be in its national interest. Russia has an intimate knowledge of the leadership in Iran and the arcane structure of power in that country. It has been and is a major provider of nuclear technology and advanced military equipment. It is all too aware of the 200 million Chinese on its eastern frontiers compared with the 20 million Russians living beyond the Urals and on the Pacific. So Russia, with its huge land boundaries, its current threats in the South, and China's increasing military assertiveness, will over time have to collaborate with the other members of the Group of Eight.

Russia knows that the Iranians are cheating, even vis-à-vis Russia. They have several thousand Russian nuclear technicians on the ground in Iran. But, they appear at this juncture unlikely to support serious sanctions at the UN Security Council. Any future deal will need to be constructed in such a way that Russia gains a great deal financially, industrially, and in terms of prestige.

But the fundamentals remain what they are. From the point of view of its national self-interest, where diplomacy must start, no nuclear power likes to see its geopolitical influence diluted by an expanded club, and Russia is no exception. The Russians also share the concern that any military intervention will be fraught with uncertain and uncontrollable consequences, including the real risk of pouring oil on the fire of Muslim fundamentalism.

Nevertheless, the Russians are still considering what approach they should take in case Iran rejects their offer of a nuclear joint venture. In

---

1 Roderic Lyne, Strobe Talbott, and Koji Watanabe, *Engaging with Russia: The Next Phase* (Washington, D.C.: Trilateral Commission, 2006).

their judgment, Iran is not afraid of economic sanctions, and they perceive a military strike as having consequences as dire for the West as for Iran. The Russians are aiming at a two-year moratorium on reprocessing and enrichment, perhaps because they are in the process of delivering their most sophisticated antiballistic missiles to the Iranians. They are doubtful that the Iranians will support this basic request as they insist on continued research on their territory. This may explain the Russians' extreme concern about the present situation.

India. India has strong geostrategic ties to Iran. This convergence was demonstrated by the jointly coordinated support from India, Russia, and Iran for the Northern Alliance in Afghanistan.

India's rate of growth and economic power are becoming formidable. In addition, it is the largest democracy in the world and, for 200 million Indians, a quasi-English-speaking democracy. Its economic ties to Iran are developing rapidly:

- India has signed a $25 billion gas contract with Iran centered on a pipeline that would pass through Pakistan;

- An ambitious steel manufacturing complex is to be built in Iran by India's giant Tata conglomerate;

- India still has a surplus of finished oil products that Iran might need; and

- From a political point of view, few in the West have focused meaningfully on the Pakistani element in the Iranians' nuclear program; these are complex and dynamic connections where India could make a significant and positive contribution.

It is interesting to note that Western statesmen keep mouthing the thought that power is shifting to Asia, but when it comes to the Iranian crisis, which is three-quarters in Asia, few senior political figures from Europe are visiting the real power centers of Delhi and Beijing.

China. With more than 100 million very poor Chinese at the doorstep of its cities; with more than 87,000 uprisings in China in 2005 mainly caused by pollution, graft, and land seizure; and with its massive problem of an aging population, China needs to achieve a rapid economic growth rate over the next decade if it wants to maintain peace on the home front. This is why it will be loath to see drastic shocks to its external energy supply or to oil prices. It is estimated that an oil price increase of $15 per barrel causes a 0.8 percent decrease in China's GDP.

China is the second-largest oil consumer in the world. It obtains 12 percent of its oil from Iran, and it has a 50 percent stake in Iran's Yavadaran, the world's largest undeveloped oil field, along with India's 20 percent.

Within that context, it is unlikely that China will support drastic actions that could ignite the fuse of a military conflagration. It stands to reason that China's Iran policy is not centered entirely on oil. Like India, China seeks a higher profile in world affairs; that means *hic et nunc* in the development of a response to the emerging Iran crisis. The Chinese would like a major role in recasting the Nuclear Non-Proliferation Treaty (NPT) so as to cope with the reality of the present geopolitical situation.

United States and Israel. The official position of the United States is that a nuclear Iran is unacceptable. As Israel puts it, "Iran creates an existential risk, the gravest risk since the creation of the state of Israel."

It is clear that the Iranian regime poses a significant threat to the United States, to its policies, and to Western interests:

- The infighting between Shia and Sunni is affecting negatively the Americans' ability to enable Iraq to make the transition to a democratic regime;

- A regional nonconventional arm race becomes more likely;

- Iran's leadership credentials in the Islamic world are becoming enhanced; thus

- The balance of soft power, and possibly soon the balance of hard power, in the Gulf could be shifting against the United States and Israel. This is important at a time when there is an anguished domestic debate in the United States about the eventual use of force against Iran. In spite of domestic support for Israel from 60 to 70 million born-again Christians, there may be, if not a rift, at least opposing tactics between the conservatives and the cautious non-interventionist side of the Bush administration. This may explain the present perception that U.S. decisiveness is at a low level at such a critical time.

Let there be no doubt, however: The United States, together with Israel, has the dominant military and intelligence power in the Persian Gulf, which has been transformed into a virtual American Gulf.

Within this context, a geostrategic question needs to be asked: Does the United States, together with Europe and Israel, have the right institutional framework within which to deal with Iran, given the tectonic changes in relative power that have taken place in the world over the past 10 years? Can the United States and Israel move forward with a soft or a hard approach without mobilizing Beijing, Delhi, Moscow, Brussels, and Tokyo, which are now additional primary players in the standoff with Iran? If they are not mobilized and if the tension escalates and erupts in an open conflict, would not the diplomatic fallout for the West, and especially for the United States and Israel, be as grave as the impact of the Suez Crisis of 1956 on Great Britain and France?

Middle East. This essay is an attempt to not only analyze the most important facets of a complex and evolving issue but also provide a framework within which to shape policies that will benefit all stakeholders.

One factor, and ultimately the decisive one, is the Middle East itself, with its growing financial wealth, population, poverty, and potential for turmoil. It is a truism to observe that the situation in the greater Middle East is volatile, with powerful undercurrents moving in conflicting directions. This has been the case for decades, but recent developments in Kashmir, Afghanistan, and Balochistan as well as in Iraq, Iran, Palestine, and Lebanon have made the social fabric of the region more vulnerable to the eruption of widespread violence. The greater Middle East has been and is in a state of fermentation. This is a critical factor in developing future recommendations designed to deal with Iran and nuclear proliferation.

Let us look at forces present in the Middle East and how they may impact alternative strategies.

Sunni countries in the Middle East believe that Tehran now sees an opportunity to export its Shia revolution to Saudi Arabia, Syria, Palestine, and Lebanon. They are all too aware of Iranian covert activities in Iraq and of their role in the "war of mosques," which could degenerate into a civil war with regional consequences. Sunni ruling classes in almost every country acknowledge that the United States constitutes the only countervailing force to stop Iran's strategy of religious conquest and political preeminence.

However, the rulers of most of these countries are caught between a rock and a hard place. Their local populations are the rock; they are disenchanted with the slow rate of progress in all avenues of civilian life. Only a small fraction of the explosion in the price of oil has benefited the masses. Improvements in health, education, justice, and social mobility have hardly percolated down to the man in the street. As a result, violence is seething below the surface, especially in densely populated areas. Hence, Ahmadinejad's declarations fall on a fertile ground, among Muslims at large.

At the other end of the spectrum, we have the ruling classes. They have a granite texture in their resilience to change. More than ever they accumulate wealth and privileges. Recent events in Palestine and Iraq have reinforced their natural propensity to maintain the status quo in most areas of political and economic life while supporting the U.S. commitment in Iraq and its strategy toward Iran as essential policies for their own survival.

Finally most of the specialists in the area acknowledge that there are no regional figures who could act as agents of change and help chart a path toward a peaceful transformation of the region. Tribal mentalities and corruption generally prevail over a regional awareness of public interest.

These comments highlight one essential fact: The area of gravest concern for the success of any U.S.-Israeli plan concerning Iran is probably the disconnect between the ruling class in the region and local populations. If surgical strikes were to become the preferred route, they might trigger generalized violence. Most observers agree that moderate regimes could be wiped out and probably replaced by "ultra" factions. Such a development could jeopardize the achievement of the twin U.S. objectives of preserving the safety of Israel and preserving a high degree of control over Middle East oil, not to mention the eradication of terrorism.

Pakistan is one country of particular concern. President Pervez Musharraf appears to have a weak grip on the military and intelligence establishment of his country, and it could grow even weaker as a result of preemptive military interventions. His demise would have far-reaching consequences and reverberations in Afghanistan, Balochistan, and on the terrorist activities of Al Qaeda.

So what should be done? The Middle East epitomizes what most countries experience in the day-to-day running of their own affairs: They are long on diagnosis and short on solutions and action.

Some Middle Eastern countries would prefer the status quo, including the continuation of protracted negotiations through the UN, for they feel that there is no efficient political alternative, such as the one outlined in the "grand bargain." Out of fear of igniting an uncontrollable chain reaction, they reject a military solution. From their vantage point, muddling through—based on the ancient conviction that in politics you do not solve problems, you survive them—is probably the least onerous approach.

Others share the conviction that "if you do not take your destiny into your hands, nobody else will." So they recommend that the United States directly enter into negotiations with the Iranians and take the leadership in developing and implementing a so-called grand bargain that meets their security concerns, those of Israel and Iran, as well as the aspirations of the local populations. They doubt that at this time either the Americans or the Iranians will move in this direction. Their reasons include the intensive mutual distrust between the United States and Iran.

If a well-publicized, good-faith approach, beneficial to all the parties concerned, fails, then a surgical strike may become unavoidable. To minimize the risk of a worst-case scenario, Middle East leaders feel that it should be immediately followed by the development and implementation of a regional framework designed to meet the security needs of the key players as well as the economic and social aspirations of the local populations, notably in the areas of water and energy. This will be essential to provide hope to the masses and a more legitimate basis upon which to construct a viable future.

Issues of Morality

All of these geostrategic considerations are in flux, complex, often contradictory, and intertwined. Just as important, they are all impacted in the global world of 2006 by moral considerations: Will a preventive strike be perceived as legitimate by the world at large? How important is such a consideration?

In today's world the level of legitimacy is, to no small extent, shaped by the verdict of the IAEA and of the UN Security Council. They currently represent the moral standards essential to generate an international consensus on whether Iran's nuclear developments represent a threat to international peace.

Nobody will deny that realpolitik still plays a role. The ambiguous positions of Russia and China, with which Iran has important trade and military links, are probably here to stay: Each has its own strategic agenda. They do not yet share the Western value system. Thus, there is a possibility that they will at the last minute sit on the fence and fail to support decisive action at the UN Security Council. In the Muslim world at large, the fear that Iran could be the catalyst to upset the power structure within Muslim communities or states is less a factor than concern over the implications of a direct military confrontation with the United States.

Internally, in Iran, the nuclear program appears to be the single most popular policy associated with the present regime, even if only because Pakistan—a Sunni state—already has nuclear weapons and because most of the leadership in Iran sees a window of opportunity to gain durable preeminence in the Middle East.

In addition, nuclear energy is viewed in the developing world as an essential alternative to oil resources, which are becoming depleted, and hence as a prerequisite to future economic development.

This reverberates in many other parts of the Muslim world, so it is doubtful whether world opinion at large would support a preemptive strike against Iran by the United States and by Israel if Iran violates IAEA injunctions. A military intervention could prove to be politically quite volatile in the current climate and much more difficult to implement than it would have been a few years ago. There could be uprisings and lasting resentment within large segments of the world population against the West unless Beijing, New Delhi, and Moscow condemn the misbehavior of Iran, which they are unlikely to do.

Issues of Tactical Implementation

Beyond world opinion, there is a third factor—the operational prospects of a preemptive strike. A preemptive strike by Israel alone looks problematic. Israeli planes would have to fly over Jordan, Iraq, and Saudi Arabia to get to Iran. Would permission be forthcoming? In addition, given the dispersion of the nuclear sites in Iran, a large aerial force—including attack aircraft, interceptors, and support aircraft—would need to fly as far as 1,700 kilometers (1,050 miles) to reach their desired targets. These targets would be difficult to hit: the most advanced Iranian missiles (Shahab-3 with a range of up to 1,900 kilometers [1,180 miles]; Ghadar with a range of 2,500–3,000 kilometers [1,550–1,860 miles]) are being built in underground townships several tens of meters below 300-meter-high (1,000 feet) mountains. The same applies to Karimi Industries, the most secretive part of the program, which deals with nuclear warheads. Striking at these underground sites may require ground forces and low-intensity nuclear weapons to destroy. Finally, there are at least 19 detected significant nuclear facilities, including Natanz and Arak. Satellite imagery, human intelligence, and the work done by the IAEA may not have yet provided a complete picture of Iran's nuclear capacity.

Nevertheless, few doubt that the United States, the "indispensable nation," together with Israel would have the military muscle and the sophistication, if there is a will, to deal a devastating blow to the existing Iranian nuclear capacity. Could they go beyond direct air force and missile strikes and commit ground troops? To a limited extent, the ability of the United States to send more soldiers to the Middle East is constrained by its budget deficit and debt ceiling, and NATO has few ground troops available, except from Turkey.

For the United States and Israel, the stakes are high. The argument in favor of a rapid, preemptive strike against Iran's perhaps imminent nuclear weapons would be that such a course of action would reduce several risks inherent in the development of a nuclear Iran:

- The risk that a nuclear Iran could be viewed, and used, by Russia and China as a powerful card to check U.S. power in the Middle East, along the present borders of Russia, and in the Far East;

- The risk that Israel's strategic primacy would be challenged with regional consequences for itself and for the United States;

- The risk that Saudi Arabia, with its Shia minority in the eastern oil-producing region (al-Hasa) could feel directly the heat of a nuclear Iran, should it, for instance, refuse to decrease production; for Saudi Arabia the Shia majority government of Iran represents its worst nightmare;

- The risk that Iran's acquisition of a nuclear weapon could encourage its neighbors, notably Saudi Arabia, Egypt, and Algeria, whose regimes may not be friendly to the West, to purchase or develop their own nuclear options; and

- The risk that Israel will survive: Iran's nuclear program combined with a radical Islamic regime and a long-range missile capability represents the biggest threat to Israel's existence since its creation.

In brief, Iran is threatening the preeminence of the United States and the process of democratization and peace in the Middle East.

It is Iran that can effectively veto movement toward peace and stability in either Palestine or Iraq through its effective support and manipulation of the political agendas of regional terrorist groups such as Hezbollah and Hamas. It is Iran that has the capacity to destabilize the flow of oil out of the Gulf.

It is Iran that determines how much of the oil and gas coming out of the Caspian basin may be safely accessed by both India and China. And it is Iran, by virtue of being one of the top five players in both oil and natural gas and a longtime diplomatic pariah as far as the United States is concerned, that offers Asian countries the best possibility for locking in long-term bilateral energy ties, a process already begun by India and China.

All these factors underpin the statement recently made by Senator John McCain (R-Ariz.): "In the end, there is only one thing worse than military action, and that is a nuclear armed Iran."

On the other hand, violently intrusive tactics can generate chain reactions that are hard to anticipate and even harder to control:

- The prospective risk of a tit for tat is evident. At the very least, the Iranian government would attempt to attack directly Israel and U.S. installations; attack neighboring oil facilities across the Gulf, disrupting oil flow to the West and Asia; block the Strait of Hormuz; engage in naval mining in the Gulf area; and trigger an explosion of Shia anger and violence across Iraq, with weapons turned against U.S. troops.

- A preventive war, even one authorized by the Security Council, could alienate a large part of the Muslim world and trigger waves of uprisings and terrorism on an unprecedented global scale against the United States, its European allies, and most powers with Muslim minorities. Attacks on targets should be expected in regions and in manners unforeseen by current defense planning. The intelligence capabilities of Iranian operatives are at a level above that of their Arab counterparts. Saudi Arabian oil installations bordering the Gulf would become obvious targets for retaliatory strikes. A successful strike could panic markets and seriously disrupt supplies of oil.

- The $500 billion U.S. investment and three years of sacrifice in Iraq could be placed at risk by Shia politicians—under pressure from mass public demonstrations—demanding the withdrawal of U.S.

forces. Upon the news of the first bombings, Shia militias could be expected to attack coalition forces in Iraq, openly threatening the current Shia-U.S. alliance in Iraq. Moktada al-Sadr, head of the Mahdi militia, publicly stated this threat during his most recent visit to Tehran.

- Oil disruptions would send markets into panic and spark short-term economic shocks. The duration of the shocks would depend completely on the success and efficiency of the military mission, yet it should be assumed that Iran would exercise its threat to cut oil exports. Oil supplies would be removed from markets for a time, either by *force majeure* or by Iran's decision. The resulting shortages would shock the global economy and encourage protests in numerous urban centers throughout the world.

- Because there are more than 20 Iranian nuclear facilities, an effective strike might require a major air force and military effort, all the more as it can be assumed that Iran would resist and attenuate their effects. The time frame needed for the strikes is in doubt. One recent analysis put forward by W. Patrick Lang, former head of Middle East intelligence at the Defense Intelligence Agency, estimates 1,000 military strike sorties.[2] This estimate would require longer than 24 hours. Should the bombing strike last more than 48 hours, the attack would be considered by the public to be a war, not a strike. No media spin would change this definition in world public opinion. Coverage by international media would unleash a negative public reaction.

The risks of significant collateral damages on civilian populations would be considerably high given the fact that many nuclear plants are close to cities; the possibility of a Chernobyl type of disaster could not be eliminated. Not only would millions of Iranian civilians be exposed to nuclear fallout (the city of Isfahan, for example), but also citizens of Bombay, Dubai, Baghdad, and other population centers might well be put at risk. The panic preceding the attack could lead to startling exoduses out of these population centers as the threat builds. Should the United States not give an ultimatum, then planners would consciously place millions at risk. The exposure of innocent civilians to radioactive fallout would also

---

2 David E. Sanger, "Why Not a Strike on Iran?" *New York Times*, January 22, 2006, Sec. 4.

receive great attention in television coverage and provoke a prolonged debate on this action. This is a neglected consideration in
the current debate over Iran and could prove to be another turning
point as significant as the Abu Ghraib scandal and the global perception of the decline of America's moral standing in the world.

- An attack might be portrayed in the world as an anti-Islamic initiative and stimulate Islamic extremists from Indonesia to Europe and
Japan. In Pakistan, the most volatile Islamic nation, mass rioting
could threaten Musharraf's tentative hold on power and even place
nuclear warheads into the hands of Islamist extremists within the
Pakistani military, triggering a response from India.

- There could be an awkward dilemma over timing unless the nuclear
weapons program was solidly and publicly provable. At present,
IAEA and Pentagon analysts estimate it will be at least 6 to 10 years
before Iran would obtain nuclear weapons capability. A U.S. or Israeli strike in the next year risks being branded as premature. As in
the case of Iraq, a vibrant debate might condemn the preemptive
U.S. or Israeli actors and redeem the Iranian regime if such an attack were to occur before all diplomatic options were exhausted.
Such an action might find its legitimacy questioned in the global
media and in the Muslim hearts and minds for years to come.
Hence, there remains a need to consider the grand bargain first
and as a real option.

- A preventive war without the seal or approval of the UN could
mark the end of the UN era. Would the United States and its allies
have the legitimacy to formulate and help implement a new set of
international governance rules after having rendered irrelevant the
rules of international law established 60 years ago?

- The permanent removal of the nuclear bomb capability in Iran might
lead to actions similar to the Iraqi pattern of imposed regime change.

- Finally, the risks of disaffection with the Bush doctrine inside the
United States would be high. The current load of U.S. security commitments worldwide is already enormous. Would the U.S. public
support their government taking on another formidable task—leading a preemptive strike against Iran's nuclear installations—with
probably little power reserve left to deal with the unexpected chain
reactions?

It is not suggested that the military option be ruled out. There is little doubt that a determined strike by missiles and aircraft could set back the Iranian nuclear weapons program by at least several years, yet it clearly might not eliminate the threat entirely. In the end, there is no guaranteed success in preventive war nor, to be objective, in the option described as the grand bargain. Such a bombing campaign might rally the country around its radical leaders. The immediate repercussions of a strike might strengthen the regime, giving the hard-liners the opportunity to eliminate numerous opposition figures within Iran. Undoubtedly, the regime would also accelerate its nuclear activities in any surviving facilities—removed from any scrutiny by IAEA inspectors—and secure nuclear weapons as soon as possible.

Thus, we have to think through with what effect, at what cost, with what coalition, and hence with what sustainability a military strike could be conducted. The balance sheet of that option can probably be established only by the United States and Israel in consultation with the EU-3. The same thought process applies to the other alternative, the diplomatic option: Can Russia, China, India, and Japan be brought to exercise responsible power over Iran if the present paradigm were to be changed? Under that assumption, could there be a different level of commitment by the leaders of the European Union?

These remarks should be complemented by two sets of facts: They concern the United States and Iran and their respective red lines.

Red lines for the United States. The United States is indeed at the center of Middle East geopolitics and to a large extent the geopolitics of the world. The United States alone has the ultimate military capacity. Having practiced superior power for the last 65 years, the United States has the resources, the knowledge, and, more important, an instinct of how to use these strengths that puts it clearly ahead of the pack. At this stage, it is essential to develop a clear understanding of where the United States presently stands:

- The United States has reached a level of military preeminence unparalleled in the history of mankind. It has developed a nuclear capacity sufficient to launch a strike guaranteed to wipe out Russia and China without the risk of suffering a return strike.

- Given this raw power and the inherent will and ability to use it, the United States is determined not to accept any policy that will force it to alter its "American way of life," predicated notably on massive domestic oil consumption, which means an increasingly heavy reliance on imports.

- There is no reason not to take the U.S. rhetoric on Iran seriously. The publication of *National Security Strategy 2006* and the declarations made in March 2006 by Vice President Cheney and Ambassador Bolton before the American Israel Public Affairs Committee confirm that this administration is determined to prevent the Iranians from deploying a nuclear bomb. The question of deployment is a significant issue for the Americans to address; it is still open and unresolved. When will Iran obtain nuclear capability? Estimates vary sharply. There is no consensus inside the U.S.–Israeli–EU-3 intelligence community.

- Finally, the U.S. administration has changed its views on the relevance and usefulness of IAEA and the UN Security Council. Deeds appear to speak louder than words. The results of President Bush's visit to India demonstrate that he is against a general principle forbidding the possession of nuclear weapons. Nuclear weapons per se are not the problem. Bad guys with nuclear weapons are. It follows that the heavyweight leaders of this administration—Cheney, Rumsfeld, Bolton, and even Rice—tend to reject the fundamental premises of the NPT. They no longer seek to create the conditions for the elimination of nuclear weapons but to eradicate the bad guys and their nuclear armament, leaving the good guys free of nuclear constraints.

Against that background, the first U.S. red line is to block the Iranian strategy to alter the balance of power in both the Gulf region and in the wider Middle East. To that effect, the United States is ready to do the heavy lifting!

Another red line for the United States is Israel. At the present time, there is a significant deepening of the U.S. defense guarantee to Israel, as expressed by President Bush to Prime Minister Ehud Olmert. This is not and will not be incorporated in the foreseeable future into a formal document, but it does represent a pronounced shift. President Bush declared that the United States will protect Israel from an Iranian attack. This may be a step toward formalizing a U.S.-Israel defense pact that would require approval by the U.S. Senate.

There are necessarily many other issues; it may be useful to mention those that are unlikely to prevent the United States from adopting a hard stance:

- **China and Russia:** Their military strength is dwarfed by that of the United States. Their internal situation is sufficiently fragile for them to want to avoid any risk of a direct confrontation with the United States.

- **Potential civilian casualties in Iran and beyond in the event of a nuclear preemptive strike on Iranian nuclear facilities:** Such considerations are traditionally of secondary importance, as illustrated by Hiroshima, Dresden, and Saint-Nazaire.

- **The religious–civil war in Iraq:** This is a significant constraint on the ability of the United States to preempt the Iranian nuclear program. Time will tell.

- **Muslim public opinion:** From a U.S. point of view, it is an issue but not an overriding one. Several hundred thousand militant Muslims residing in the United States have been asked to leave the country, and the protection of U.S. embassies and other installations will be reinforced

Red lines for Iran. Above all, the clerical regime of Iran wants to survive. Iran's leadership became nervous when U.S. troops landed to the west (Iraq) and to the east (Afghanistan) of Iran. The clerical regime includes three pragmatic factional power blocs—those led by Mehdi Karroubi, Mostapha Moin, and Hashemi Rafsanjani, the leader of the unelected Expediency Council. They all continue to openly criticize the president. He is increasingly viewed as a loose cannon. His messianic claims have proved more controversial in Iran than in the West. Among the president's critics, dealmaker Rafsanjani may be a significant figure for he represents the business class and the unelected clerics. The three factions may be willing to engage in an opening to the United States for, in contrast to Ahmadinejad, they do not thrive on a siege mentality or on provoking a clash with the West.

We must then ask the question: What would be the red lines for the conservative pragmatists? There are no sure answers until real negotiations take place, but we have indications. They are likely to be:

1. Assured territorial integrity;
2. Security guarantees from the United States and Israel;

3.   Lifting of U.S. sanctions;

4.   Assurances of foreign investment with a focus on the oil sector;

5.   Support of World Trade Organization membership for Iran;

6.   Repatriation of Iranian funds frozen in U.S. banks since 1979;

7.   Continued nuclear research, with IAEA inspections; and

8.   Designation of the Mujahedin-e Khalq as a terrorist organization.

So it may be worth raising the question: In a situation of that significance and volatility, where there are new primary players that have emerged and that have thus far played an undervalued role, are unilateralism and the extreme use of force the most effective ways of dealing with all aspects of the Iranian issue? Should we not investigate and rejuvenate the diplomatic option?

Can Diplomacy and Creative Compromise Be an Alternative?

The diplomatic option needs to be further explored and enlarged as long as the military option remains plausible and constitutes the *ultima ratio* in case diplomacy does not bear fruit.

This implies that the United States and the West must be ready to recognize the new geopolitical landscape and to move with China, India, and Russia to convince Iran of the red lines of the United States and the West. Direct dialogue, time, and strength are essential ingredients to help change public opinion and leaders' convictions on the other side of the negotiating table. Slowly but unavoidably, the United States and the West will have to draw the practical conclusions of the 2006 reality: There is a new balance of power emerging. The *nomenklatura* of China, Russia, and Iran have fundamental points in common. They are in search of national preeminence in their traditional areas of influence. Of equal importance is the protection of the personal interests of a few hundred robber barons who make up the national oligarchies. To a large extent they have captured the state wealth of their own countries. The ideology and the propaganda used by each leadership to protect their individual positions vary according to history, culture, and expediency.

Within that context, three observations are relevant. First, the leaders of these three nations are there to stay and will pay to preserve their power. In the seventeenth and eighteenth centuries, the kings of France devoted 10 to 12 percent of the country's GDP to finance the army and police. Today the figure is about 1.5 to 2 percent. Today in China, Russia, and Iran, 10 to 15 percent of GDP is the amount needed in order to maintain law and order and eventually project power outside of one's frontiers. These expenditures benefit small minorities that are getting immensely rich while the majorities still labor in relative poverty.

Second, the leaderships of these countries will prefer jaw-jaw to war-war, for the latter alternative entails considerable risks for themselves personally. The members of the *nomenklatura* continue to be keenly interested in creating more wealth, provided they can keep the bulk for themselves. They favor trade as a means to generate new resources, but they will make sure that the masses get only the crumbs. They are also motivated by national pride and by the search for regional preeminence. They have a high sense of insecurity and a vivid recollection of external interventions that took place at regular intervals over the past 75 years.

China is a case at point. It illustrates the fact that a large measure of free trade and rapid industrialization is still compatible with a ruthlessly autocratic regime.

Today, most experts would agree that sanctions on Iran are unlikely to succeed. Trading remains a step in the right direction to promote "the forward strategy of freedom" even if the ultimate goal may take decades to be reached. Recent history has taught us that the more developing countries are richly endowed with oil, the slower the pace of progress toward democracy. Their leadership can afford the military paraphernalia necessary to keep the lid on the masses.

This seems to be the real world of today, and it could be here to stay. In addition, we have to keep in mind the experience gathered in Afghanistan and Iraq that illustrates the complexities of inducing major political and social changes from the outside. Within that context, a grand bargain may appear a realistic option, a practical step forward in a long process of a mutation of mentalities. It need not be interpreted as a retreat by the United States from the project of democratic transformation of the Middle East but as an initiative from the sole military superpower in the world to develop and implement a twenty-first-century concept for international security over one or two generations. Such an option would be, in a way, the child of the international institutions created after World War II, essentially by the United States.

We are aware that this experiment was tried a decade ago with North Korea in the context of the Korean Peninsula Energy Development Organization (KEDO) and that the results left much to be desired, but times have changed. There have been fewer cross-border conflicts over the last 20 years than at any time over the last two centuries, and the aspiration for peace is universal.

The diplomatic strategy still being applied in Northeast Asia vis-à-vis the North Korean nuclear threat remains a case in point. The six-party talks have engaged the belligerent, erratic North Korean state in a series of negotiations with direct neighbors and regional powers. We should ask whether this diplomatic option offers a precedent that can be applied to Iran to allow its regime the mechanism to save face by widening the negotiations to include the Asian giants—with whom its future is strategically tied—and not only with Europeans who may be seen as symbols of a colonial past.

The world is longing for peace, economic growth, and the eradication of extreme poverty. So it may be ripe for a grand bargain with Iran initiated and led by the United States, supported by Europe, Russia, Japan, China, and India—as it seems unlikely that the UN will reform itself within the necessary time frame to lead such a project.

Finally, one should continue to support a UN solution provided it has real teeth in it. But the likelihood of such an occurrence remains to be seen. This is why a grand bargain will need to be essentially political but with an economic dimension.

The Political Dimension

The political dimension presupposes that the United States engages directly in a dialogue with Iran and abandons the rhetoric of regime change. The United States should also recognize the fact that a bilateral diplomatic solution in the case of Iran will not succeed and that a multilateral approach—taking into account the interests of the most relevant parties concerned as well as the Persian mentality—will be necessary to move forward toward a lasting, peaceful solution.

What is needed is the creation of a regional Middle East nuclear council composed of countries that have the nuclear bomb or have the imminent capacity to develop it and that have a close economic and political relationship with Iran. The list comprises the United States, Russia, Israel, Iran, China, India, Pakistan, Japan, the United Kingdom, and France.

Key components of the grand bargain:

- The United States would exploit fully the best possible "second tracks" to indicate a U.S. preparedness to enter into negotiations aimed at an agreement with Tehran.

- The regional nuclear council would be established with the visible support of all of the above countries.

- All parties would agree to freeze at present levels their existing capacity to produce nuclear bombs.

- All 10 countries would agree on a wide range of measures to prevent proliferation of all materials involved in the production of nuclear bombs and would provide effective implementation of such policies.

- All parties would agree to a process to neutralize risks of regional nuclear conflicts—putting into place an early warning system and insuring that the regional nuclear council is the hub for crisis management and has the capacity to develop a common strategic analysis of potential conflicts between existing nuclear powers.

- Israel should be provided with a comprehensive security package by both the United States and Europe, as defined within Article 5 of the NATO charter.

- Iran would be offered explicit U.S. security guarantees.

- Russia would be offered a nuclear cooperation agreement with the United States.

- The Montreux Convention would be enlarged to cover the demilitarization of the Strait of Hormuz.

- Iran, and possibly other countries such as Turkey, Algeria, and Saudi Arabia, would be guaranteed a supply of nuclear fuel (the fuel banks) for peaceful nuclear applications. As a Chinese wall cannot exist between peaceful nuclear energy and weapons development, there must be unrestricted access for all IAEA inspection teams to Iranian nuclear facilities.

- IAEA would continue to play a critical role in a control capacity.

The Economic Dimension
It is proposed that, concomitant with the creation of a regional nuclear council, a range of economic measures be taken involving the Trilat-

eral countries and the wealthiest oil-producing countries in the Middle East to promote trade and investment in the region's least developed countries such as Palestine, Jordan, Tunisia, Morocco, Turkey, Egypt, and Algeria. Over the long term, this would probably be the safest approach to promote security and enhance the chances of a gradual transformation toward more democracy. Within that context, unequivocal support should be given to help these countries access the World Trade Organization and create development banks and microcredit institutions that would benefit the masses directly by enhancing their infrastructures as well as their health and educational levels. In that area, a leading role should be played by Saudi Arabia, the United Arab Emirates, the European Development Bank, and other leading private and public institutions.

A regional Middle East water council should also be established to discuss the distribution of the region's rarest resource. Such a council might serve to diffuse potential conflicts—"water wars"—that are plausible in the near future. Countries to be included would be Turkey, Syria, Lebanon, Iraq, Israel, Palestine, and Jordan. Such a regional cooperation council would instill a focus on interdependency that is lacking in the Middle East, one of the few regions in the world without a regional body (the Arab League is simply not capable of dealing with such a critical issue as water without Turkey's or Israel's participation). As coal and steel agreements eventually led to a united Europe, regional initiatives in water and oil, under a comprehensive security umbrella, could redefine and integrate the Middle East.

Conclusion

In conclusion, we acknowledge that:

Iran's present policies, which may well worsen in the near future, are a direct threat to Europe because of the advancement of its nuclear missile program, because an Iranian nuclear capacity in the hands of a theocracy could radicalize the Middle East and segments of the Muslim population in Europe, and because the emergence of nuclear powers in this part of the world could generate turmoil in the production and distribution of oil with the corresponding impact on world economic expansion. It is indeed a special challenge to Europe; the European Union has a population of 12 million Muslims with a strong extremist minority and complex, ancient links with the Middle East. Its natural proclivity could be appeasement, to avoid at all cost any type of military confrontation, but the Europeans need to recognize that there could be circumstances under which a military option would better serve the objectives of peace.

Iran is a threat to the long-term strategy of the United States, which is still deeply engaged in Iraq and which seeks to transform the Middle East through democratization. Just as important is the U.S. perception of its national interests and its recognition that it has the overwhelming military power to pursue them on its own.

Iran is a threat to Russia, Japan, South Korea, and Southeast Asia because of their economic ties to Iran, Muslim minorities in their regions, and the possibility of the disruption of oil deliveries.

Iran is a challenge to the free world's battle against terror, the proliferation of weapons of mass destruction, and extreme poverty. It is a challenge to the world at large and, notably, to China, India, and Russia in their struggles to develop their own paths to democratization (China and Russia) and economic prosperity.

The key issue, outside the UN process, is how to deal with a threat of that complexity and magnitude. The realistic answer is probably that all three options should be pursued in a concomitant, complementary, and convincing way, with the ultimate aim to implement a grand bargain that meets the strategic, security, and economic objectives of the primary players and of the world at large. There is a scenario in which preemptive strikes against Iran may be a necessity, much as it may be against Iran's national interest. We all know that a war, even a limited one, could foster more violence in the Middle East; in Iran and Afghanistan; in Asia; and at home in Europe. It could raise oil prices to recession levels. All these are powerful arguments against the use of the military option, but they do not come close to matching the case of stopping a regime if it continues to be clearly bent on eradicating Israel and the West.

The risks and costs of a military intervention are such that they put a premium on intensive and creative diplomacy. The United States must take the lead. The Europeans must be involved. The Russians, Chinese, and Indians must be given a taste of what is in it for them in order to persuade them to play a primary role. Other Middle Eastern countries are obvious stakeholders. At the outset, everybody must agree to put ideology aside and take a long-term view. We all know that feudal societies endowed with oil evolve politically at a slow pace. They are unlikely to convert to democracy overnight. At the same time, all parties must understand the others' red lines. In the case of the West, there should be no doubt in anybody's mind that a threat against Israel would trigger a cataclysmic U.S. and Western response.

Finally, the United States must realize the limits of unilateralism and of its monopoly over hard power. To address the Iranian issue this year and over the next decade will require U.S. leadership to carefully blend hard and soft power. The campaign for democracy in the Arab World may, over time, bear unpredictable fruit, as is the case in Palestine. Intimacy among the Trilateral countries may become a critical factor to success. The United States may need to recognize the benefits of European values and of the EU experiment. The United States should leverage the experience and financial resources of other Middle Eastern countries. It must give China, India, and Russia the right level of recognition in terms of power, status, and responsibility, as they deserve, and it should educate key nations around the world to the U.S. change of heart on the NPT.

In brief, the United States must lead an alliance in which it shares power rather than launches a crusade. It must encourage Asian and Western leadership to reach out to the various pragmatist power blocs in Iran. It must give them the hope of long-term survival, with the all-important assurance of growth, security, and economic renewal for Iran. Finally, it must count on the forces of global information and on the example of successful transitions to democracy to make the seeds of change grow in closed countries and societies. In brief, the United States must be in the vanguard of creative diplomacy to achieve those of its national and international objectives that are basically shared by its Trilateral partners.

3

Iran Case Study: Time Is Running Out

Thérèse Delpech

Throughout much of the 1990s, the assessment of the Iranian nuclear program differed on the two sides of the Atlantic. For the United States, a high priority had been to convince its European allies and the International Atomic Energy Agency (IAEA) that Iran was engaged in illicit nuclear activities. But by then, Europe had adopted a policy dubbed "critical dialogue" with Tehran—which was hardly critical on the nuclear issue—and European capitals did not pay much attention to the warnings of the Clinton administration. The IAEA, for its part, was at the time deeply engaged in Iraq and never found the information provided by Washington on Iran convincing enough to prompt a thorough investigation on Iranian territory. Visits—as opposed to inspections—were suggested by Tehran to solve the problem, and they were accepted by the IAEA's director, Hans Blix. Those visits did allow some suspected sites to be seen without ever providing the conclusive evidence that Iran was concealing nuclear activities from the IAEA. This period now deserves to be reassessed since Iran apparently restarted its nuclear program in 1985, in the middle of the Iran-Iraq war.[1]

At the same time, there was another major U.S. goal concerning Iran: stopping external assistance, and particularly Russian assistance,

---

1 This date is obviously of great significance. At the time, there was no nuclear power plant whatsoever in Iran and, as a result, no need for nuclear fuel. But the war with Iraq was pitiless, and chemical weapons had been used since 1983 against Iranian troops, leaving, to this day, deep scars in the Iranian national psyche. Research on uranium enrichment centrifuge technology started in 1985, and key design technology and sample centrifuge components were purchased from the A. Q. Khan network in 1987.

to Iran's nuclear program as well as to long-range ballistic missiles.[2] The Russian ministry in charge of nuclear energy (Minatom) had extensive relations with Iran, and the exact nature of the deals between Moscow and Tehran was under question. This cooperation was thought to be much more ambitious than simply interactions related to nuclear power reactors and fuel supply.[3] Such suspicions were in fact warranted since Boris Yeltsin did acknowledge confidential agreements with Tehran and even promised to stop them. Whether he fully succeeded in this endeavor is still in doubt. One may even question the completeness of the knowledge acquired by the IAEA concerning past Iranian-Russian cooperation: Russia may still fear that the full extent of its deals with Tehran will surface. But that Russia became a progressively more responsible partner is generally thought to be an acceptable judgment since 2002–03.[4] Taking into account Moscow's weapons sales to Iran as late as 2006, one might wonder whether this judgment is accurate.

This ambiguous situation could have lasted many more years if the Iranian opposition in exile, National Council of Resistance of Iran (NCRI), most probably taking advantage of the presence of informers within the country, had not decided to give a sensational press conference in Washington in August 2002.[5] At that time, two important Iranian nuclear sites were revealed: Natanz and Arak. In addition, the

---

2 There may still be a number of undisclosed transfers from Russia and from the former USSR (Ukraine, for instance) to Iran in the 1990s. Part of the Russian knowledge and technology may also have been acquired through North Korea.

3 In the 1990s, Tehran reportedly made a bargain with Moscow whereby Iranian restraint in the Caucasus would allow Iran to gain access to Russian weapons and technology.

4 In August 1992, Russia and Iran signed an agreement for bilateral nuclear cooperation, and in January 1995 another specific agreement was signed by the two nations concerning the Bushehr nuclear power plant. In a secret protocol to this agreement, Russia offered to supply a large research reactor and a centrifuge enrichment plant. After President Clinton complained to President Yeltsin, fuel assistance was cancelled. Despite the official ban, technical assistance continued to be provided to Iran. This assistance helped Iran, inter alia, in the following domains: heavy-water production plant, heavy-water research reactor, industrial-scale uranium milling facility, laser enrichment pilot plant.

5 It would have been sensational because of its immediate and long-term consequences, not because of its attendance.

existence of a front company by the name of Kalaye Electric was also said to be providing cover for nuclear activities undertaken in Natanz.[6] The IAEA requested access to those sites in September, but the inspection initially foreseen in October 2002 finally took place only at the end of February 2003.[7] The first site proved to be related to uranium enrichment (two plants were under construction: a pilot fuel enrichment plant and a large commercial-scale fuel enrichment plant; both were declared to the IAEA for the first time during this visit). The second site was devoted to the production of heavy water, which is used in reactors producing weapons-grade plutonium (it is remarkable that under comprehensive Nuclear Non-Proliferation Treaty [NPT] safeguards agreements, heavy-water production facilities are not classified as nuclear facilities and thus are not required to be declared to the IAEA).

The two routes to the bomb were therefore justifiably supposed to be progressing. The IAEA reported in June 2003 that centrifuges were being installed at Natanz near a vast underground facility now heavily protected and a heavy-water reactor was under construction in Arak.[8]

During the February 2003 visit, IAEA inspectors requested but were denied access to the front company called Kalaye Electric, which was said to be related to the nuclear program in some unspecified way and where they intended to take environmental samples. The Iranian authorities considered such visits as being obligatory only with an Additional Protocol in force. At the time, Iran acknowledged only that the workshop had been used for the production of centrifuge components but stated that there had been no testing of these components involving the use of nuclear material, either at the Kalaye Electric Company or at any other location in Iran. As early as October 2003, however,

---

6 In 1995, Iran moved the research program from the Tehran Nuclear Technology Centre to a secret location at the Kalaye Electric Company, located in Tehran's suburbs, presumably to reduce the risk of detection by IAEA inspectors.

7 Iran took advantage of the mounting international confrontation with Iraq following the passage of UN Security Council resolution 1441 (November 2002) to postpone the IAEA inspection. The focus on Iraq obviously gave Iran some breathing room at that time.

8 On April 11, Iran's vice president and atomic energy chief, Gholam Reza Aghazadeh, said Iran was "determined" to complete work within three years on the heavy-water reactor in Arak, which could produce plutonium for a nuclear weapon.

Gholam Reza Aghazadeh, head of the Atomic Energy Organization of Iran (AEOI) since 1997 and vice president of the Islamic Republic of Iran, acknowledged that Iran had carried out testing of centrifuges at the Kalaye Electric Company using UF6 between 1998 and 2002.

Tehran also claimed that its enrichment program was entirely indigenous, an assertion that also had to be corrected at a later stage, when traces of low-enriched uranium (LEU) and highly enriched uranium (HEU) were found on Iranian territory. Then, what was suddenly essential to underline was not the indigenous nature of the program but the exact opposite: the foreign origin of the "contamination." This issue is still partially unresolved in 2006.[9] Last but not least, in February 2003, Iran acknowledged for the first time the receipt in 1991 of natural uranium in the form of UF6, UF4 and UO2, stored at a previously undisclosed location (JHL at the Tehran Nuclear Research Centre). According to Iran, most of the UF4 had been converted by Iran into uranium metal in 2000, information that was going to receive a large number of comments in the following months—and years.[10]

From February 2003 onward a number of safeguard issues needed to be clarified in connection with the implementation of the agreement between Iran and the IAEA. Therefore, after this time the IAEA undertook intensive verification activities. This was particularly necessary since, in addition to the IAEA inspections and reports, a number of countries—including European countries—had troubling information concerning purchases (or often only attempted purchases) on their own territory that could hardly be explained by a civilian program.[11]

It is unfortunate that access to Natanz was not obtained until February 2003 and to Kalaye Electric until mid-2003 because of Iran's persistent delaying tactics. What was done by Iran during this crucial period is still an important part of the not entirely solved equation. One

---

9 In the February 2006 IAEA director general's report, it is stated: "The origin of some HEU particles, and of the LEU particles, remains to be further investigated" and "It is difficult to establish a definitive conclusion with respect to all of the contamination."

10 China was the discreet supplier of the undeclared natural uranium in the form of UF6, UF4, and UO2.

11 In fact, Iran has proved able to import dual-use items from a number of foreign sources, including various types of computer-controlled machine tools, balancing machines, vacuum pumps, high-strength aluminum, maraging steel, and electron beam welders.

can only make the following hypothesis: Documents and equipment may have been secured; some sites may have been cleaned (as was inter alia the case at Kalaye Electric and the laser enrichment [atomic vapor laser isotope separation (AVLIS)] facility at Lashkar Abad); experts may have been told what had been officially decided to tell inspectors; and, finally, important evidence may have been removed. On the other hand, it was pretty clear to international inspectors when they arrived at Natanz that one major goal of the Iranians was to convince them that they were advanced enough in their uranium enrichment project and there was no way to stop it. (The program consisted of a practically complete front end of a nuclear fuel cycle, including uranium mining and milling, conversion, enrichment, fuel fabrication, heavy-water production, a light-water reactor, a heavy-water-research reactor, and associated research and development (R&D) facilities).

Such has been Tehran's strategy since then. According to Iranian authorities, no nation and no international pressure will be able to stop Iran's nuclear program because it is too advanced. This position was repeated again in June 2006 after the offer proposed by the UN Perm-5 + Germany to Iran.

However, even with the handicap of late inspections, major violations were discovered by the IAEA between February and September 2003. Undeclared nuclear material, undeclared nuclear sites, and undeclared nuclear activities were surfacing while evolving stories were provided by Iran to explain from one inspection to the next what was being discovered.

Eighteen years of concealment were finally disclosed, and this was more than enough to justify a strong resolution at the board meeting of September 2003, requesting the director general to submit a full report to the next board meeting in November, "enabling the Board to draw definitive conclusions."[12] This resolution, inter alia, called on Iran to provide accelerated cooperation and full transparency to ensure that there were no further failures to report material, facilities, and activities that Iran was obliged to report, and to suspend all further uranium enrichment–related activities and any reprocessing activities. Two and a half years later, full cooperation and transparency are still wanting.

---

12 "Implementation of the NPT Safeguards Agreement in the Islamic Republic of Iran," doc. no. GOV/2003/69, IAEA Board of Governors, September 12, 2003, www.iaea.org/Publications/Documents/Board/2003/gov2003-69.pdf.

By the autumn of 2003, it was clear that the "breaches" (a term equivalent to "violations") of the obligation to comply were significant enough to justify referral to the United Nations Security Council (UNSC). They were described in the following way in November 2003: (1) failure to report the use of imported natural UF6 for the testing of centrifuges at the Kalaye Electric Company in 1999 and 2002; (2) failure to report the import of natural uranium metal in 1994 and its subsequent transfer for use in laser enrichment experiments; (3) failure to report the production of UO2, UO3 and UF4; (4) failure to report the separation of plutonium; (5) and failure to provide design information for the centrifuge testing facility at the Kalaye Electric Company, for the laser laboratories in Tehran and Lashkar Ab'ad, for the facilities involved in the production of nuclear material, and for the hot cell facility where the plutonium separation took place.

The Europeans decided to intervene just a month earlier in order to find a diplomatic solution to the mounting crisis. The three capitals (Berlin, London, and Paris) initially came together for a number of reasons: They wanted to show that negotiations could succeed in hindering proliferation; they were anxious to find some unity after the dispute over Iraq in the spring of 2003; and they actually also felt threatened by Iranian nuclear and ballistic missile programs. After all, the first Shehab-3 test had been a surprise for everybody concerned, and the ranges were constantly increasing. The main idea provided by Berlin, London, and Paris was—in line with the September IAEA resolution—to suspend (and eventually to put an end to) concealed activities that could give Iran the ability to produce weapons-grade materials. The explicit counterpart was to suspend any referral to the UNSC of the Iranian dossier while the suspension of the fuel cycle remained in place in Iran.[13]

Whether the Europeans succeeded in giving credibility to "effective multilateralism," an expression present in the EU Common Strategy on Weapons of Mass Destruction, should now be assessed. As of May 2006, just before the Perm-5 + 1 offer that was presented to Iran by

---

13 The fear was that any premature referral to the UNSC would leave the
    Security Council divided and ineffective. In late spring 2006, one may
    question whether the delay did not simply allow Iran to gain time,
    without achieving any additional consensus among the major players
    at the UNSC over the years.

the three European countries, China, Russia, and the United States, the result did not appear very encouraging:

- Two agreements (October 21, 2003[14] and November 15, 2004) have been violated by Tehran;

- Progress has been made on key components of the nuclear program (not only according to two major negotiators of the former team under former president Mohammad Khatami—Sirus Nasseri and Hassan Rohani—who both wrote before July 2005 that the negotiations with the Europeans allowed Iran to gain precious time, but also in conformity with the actual pace of centrifuge assembly and production of enriched uranium in March and April 2006);

- A radical and unpredictable president was elected in June 2005, contrary to most expectations;

- Iranian officials now describe their nuclear program as "irreversible" and declare that Iran can soon become "a superpower";

- Iran has drastically curtailed cooperation with nuclear inspectors;

- The international community, as we used to call it, is not a bit closer to either understanding the seriousness of the situation or reacting to it in a proper fashion: in March, a lengthy struggle began in the UNSC over how to respond to Iran's defiance. The eight-page IAEA report produced on April 28 at the request of the UNSC may have documented (1) a blunt refusal by Tehran to accede to the UNSC's demands, (2) significant progress on enrichment and new questions concerning P2 centrifuges and plutonium, and (3) an increasing difficulty in monitoring Iran's nuclear activities, but it did not change the reluctance of China and Russia to adopt a mandatory order to Iran.[15]

---

14 This agreement was, at the time, considered by the Europeans as "a last chance" for Iran to accept the board's demands. Two and a half years later, the Board of Governors' demands are still not met. Nor are the UNSC demands. But who cares?

15 Russia and China continue balking at the use of Chapter VII of the UN charter. "We all know what Chapter VII involves," said Wang Guanya, China's ambassador to the United Nations and president of the UNSC in April. "All we want is a diplomatic solution, so therefore I believe that by involving Chapter VII, it will be more complicated." No one asked him which step should now be adopted instead, in order for a "diplomatic solution" to succeed.

This reluctance by the international community is still present at the end of June, as the agreement reached in Vienna on June 1 was related essentially to incentives, not to sanctions.

European Goals—and Results

What was remarkable in the European initiative, according to most observers, was the unity of the three European capitals during the whole period. Tensions have occurred from time to time, but they never surfaced in such a way that Tehran could exploit them. However, while the performance is significant for European Union external policy, the main problem is not so much whether the EU-3 maintained their unity as whether they succeeded in achieving their goals.

Such European goals could be described in the following way:

Keep open the option of a favorable political change in Iran that would lead Tehran to accept a deal with the West whereby sensitive nuclear fuel cycle activities that could support a nuclear weapons program would be abandoned in exchange for economic and security benefits as well as fuel supply guarantees. The opposite happened with the election of Mahmoud Ahmadinejad, the most unlikely partner for any kind of compromise, particularly for anything related to what is considered to belong to national security. The idea that a deal could be concluded with President Mohammad Khatami or, perhaps—with even more authority—with President Ali Akbar Hashemi Rafsanjani[16] was not unreasonable (although Rafsanjani was heavily involved in the Iranian nuclear program during the 1990s). One can even contend that it may have been a lost opportunity for all concerned and, in particular, for the United States.[17]

But the new president is a man of confrontation and appears to have been chosen for this very reason by the core of the Iranian regime: Supreme Leader Ayatollah Ali Hoseini-Khamenei and the Pasdaran. As mayor of Tehran, he was famous for having personally opposed a

---

16 It is worth noting that President Rafsanjani, when elected president in August 1989, embarked on a more ambitious nuclear program with potential military applications.

17 According to a number of open sources, Washington and Tehran have periodically held secret talks (in Geneva, New York, and other places) on issues of common concern since the September 2001 terrorist attacks.

demand from Cairo to change the name of Islambuli Street and to withdraw the picture of President Sadat's murderer from a public site, at a time when Egypt was seeking normal, bilateral diplomatic relations with Tehran at the ambassadorial level. Mahmoud Ahmadinejad apparently considered the murderer as an inspiration for Iranian youth.

Ahmadinejad's repeated, outrageous words regarding Israel, calling it a "tumor" that should be "wiped off the map," gives an idea of the new president's radical thinking. The statement having been made in the midst of an international crisis over the Iranian nuclear program, it also shows Ahmadinejad's lack of concern for the reaction of the outside world.[18] In April 2006, after demonstrating the ability to enrich uranium in Natanz, Iran wanted the whole world to recognize that "the facts on the ground have changed," as if Tehran would be able to decide alone a new status quo that the UNSC should only accept as a fact, whatever its demands in the March presidential statement. In addition, the country's spiraling militarism—trumpeted in missile tests and military maneuvers[19]—makes the international community uneasy and the whole Middle East region more nervous than it already was before June 2005. For most Arab nations—not just for Turkey and Israel—Tehran is moving in a very worrying direction because of military reasons and because it has sought to exploit unrest within the Shia populations in the Gulf states.

To make a long story short, the political change was far worse than any observer—from within the region or from abroad—had anticipated. As long as Mahmoud Ahmadinejad is in place, and as long as his confrontational attitude prevails, flexibility, compromise and negotiations are not in the cards. To make a deal or a bargain, one needs a partner, and he is definitely not a possible one. The only deal he could apparently agree to is to get both talks and nuclear activities on Iranian soil.

---

18 On April 25, again the Iranian president insisted, "Israel cannot continue to live."

19 Military maneuvers took place from March 31 to April 6 in the Gulf of Oman and the Strait of Hormuz. The exercises included some 17,000 troops from all of Iran's armed services, including the Islamic Revolutionary Guard and the Basij militia. A series of missiles was presented, supposed to achieve "revolutionary technological leaps." Some experts underlined that the Iranians are known to exaggerate their technical capabilities. Still, it was clear that Iran was increasing its weapons systems by both foreign and indigenous measures.

So a major objective should be to make Ayatollah Ali Khamenei wonder whether the price Iran would have to pay for such confrontational tactics will not be too high.[20] As of April 2006 no action has been taken in this direction by the international community. To the contrary: So far, Iran has had no price at all to pay. As a result, the regime feels reinforced rather than weakened.[21] How to contain Iran's nuclear ambitions has now been the subject of a second round of discussions at the UNSC in April 2006, leading to a new offer, this time clearly supported by the United States, presenting a last choice to Tehran. In case of refusal, new measures would be contemplated at the UNSC. Iran may vow to resist any international pressure, but it remains to be seen whether and for how long the Iranian government's intransigence will persist if serious pressure is applied. This has not even been tried yet.

Better understand the nature of the Iranian nuclear program by securing Tehran's commitment to further international inspections and verification activities. This second goal has been largely attained. In 2006, the level of knowledge acquired about the Iranian nuclear program is considerable, even if major questions remain concerning such issues as the origin of LEU and HEU particle contamination found at various locations in Iran; the extent of Iran's efforts to import, manufacture, and use centrifuges of P1 and—even more—P2 designs; the 1987 Pakistani offer (A. Q. Khan's clandestine network); the plutonium separation experiments after 1993; production of polonium 210 and beryllium; and the nature of the nuclear activities conducted on the military site identified by the IAEA at Lavizanshian.

The fact that Iran had failed in a number of instances over an extended period of time to meet its obligations under its IAEA safeguards agreement is no longer debated: as early as June 2003, the IAEA re-

---

20 The supreme leader appears closer to the ideologists on the nuclear issue. Ali Larijani and Mahmoud Ahmadinejad feel they have no domestic constraint, and their approach has gained benefits so far (conversion has been restarted with no consequences and enrichment with a weak reaction from the UNSC).

21 There may be a consensus in Iran concerning the civilian nuclear program, but there is none on building nuclear weapons that many Iranians fear would harm Iran's national interest by making it a target of international pressure and steering it back to the isolation of the early 1980s, a period of radical absolutes that Mahmoud Ahmadinejad frequently invokes as an ideal.

ported Iran's past failures "to report material, facilities and activities as required by its safeguards obligations" and additional breaches have regularly been identified by the agency since then. In addition, since Tehran's recognition that it has received the necessary technology for casting and machining uranium metal into hemispherical forms, the NPT has been violated as well (Article II stipulates that "each non-nuclear weapon State Party to the Treaty undertakes not to . . . seek or receive any assistance in the manufacture of nuclear weapons or other nuclear explosive devices").

The international verification activities have become increasingly difficult in Iran, and this is an additional justification for making mandatory under Chapter VII the UNSC demands if the Perm-5 + 1 offer is not accepted by Tehran. Since February 2006, Iran has put an end to the implementation of the Additional Protocol—which has never been ratified by Tehran—contrary to the requests by the IAEA Board of Governors and the UNSC. The agency is now confined to the implementation of the safeguards agreement and, as a result, its ability to clarify outstanding issues or to confirm the absence of undeclared materials and activities has been curtailed.

As explained below, Iran may be closer to its first nuclear weapon than most observers anticipated only a year ago. Time is running out, and so far the tempo of diplomacy has been far too slow to convince Iran to change its course. The most recent diplomatic initiative (on June 1, 2006) may only confirm this analysis because Tehran did not provide any answer at the end of the month, which was the deadline. On June 30, during a Group of Eight (G-8) ministerial meeting in Moscow, the deadline was extended until mid-July.

Delay the Iranian nuclear program through the suspension of major activities related to the fuel cycle, with the idea that the first goal would eventually be attained.[22] This remains to be assessed properly. As strange as it may sound, whether the suspension has actually delayed the Iranian nuclear program is debatable. As indicated earlier, in December 2004, Sirus Nasseri declared in an interview that the es-

---

22 The EU3 initially (in 2003) wanted to obtain an explicit "permanent cessation" of the fuel cycle activities, but in response to Iranian opposition, they dropped any reference to it, while making clear that "satisfactory assurances" actually meant "permanent cessation." In the battle of words, Iran has always been stronger and more astute than the European negotiators.

sence of Iranian planning since 2002, when the nuclear program was unveiled, was to gain time to work without threats of any kind from the UNSC while continuing to make progress on issues where the technical knowledge was still insufficient: "Of course, we could also have made progress while confronting the world, but our task would have been more difficult and we would have lost control over the timing."[23]

The Iranian idea was to suspend what could be suspended in order to work in peace, and only for as long as the technical problems remained to be solved. From this perspective, one should remember that conversion activities were not included in the first agreement with the Europeans, that Iran never stopped working on centrifuge assembly at a small level, and that their centrifuge production activity has remained largely unverified.

This probably explains why, contrary to expectations, Tehran was able in March 2006 to assemble rapidly—and to operate successfully with UF6—164 centrifuges, a major step in the direction of the completion of the pilot plant at Natanz. In May 2006, three cascades were assembled. At this pace, a pilot plant of 1,000 centrifuges could be in place by the end of the year. And the Shehab-3 missile[24]—displayed at military parades in Tehran and under the control of the Iranian Revolutionary Guards and the Iranian air force—has the payload capacity and the airframe diameter to carry a nuclear warhead.[25] There are two models of the Shehab-3: an old model shaped like a cone, and a new model—the baby-bottle design—with a tri-cone design. In addition, there are reports that Iran recently bought from North Korea a new missile known as the BM-25 (a variation of the old Soviet SSN6), which has a range of 2,500 to 3,000 kilometers (1,550 to 1,865 miles) and is definitely a nuclear missile.

---

23 *Sharg*, December 5–6, 2004.

24 In September 2005, Iran displayed six Shehab-3 missiles, but experts consider it prudent to assume that Iran has several dozen of such missiles in its arsenal. Tehran seems to have mastered the liquid fuel technology and is now moving to solid fuel. The missile is mobile and easy to hide. Apparently, the Arrow system deployed in Israel was specifically designed against the Shehab-3.

25 On August 11 and October 20, 2004, Iran test-launched a new version of the Shehab-3 with a smaller diameter and a conically shaped nose. The redesign shows that Iran has made great technological advances in its missile program, with or without foreign assistance.

Achieve a wide international consensus on the assessment of Iranian nuclear ambitions and the need to stop them. The IAEA reports have produced a wide consensus concerning the real nature of the Iranian nuclear ambitions. A February 2006 IAEA report underlines that after three years of intense inspection efforts, "The Agency is waiting for Iran to address the topics which could have a military dimension."[26] The formula has been inserted in the presidential statement issued by the UNSC on March 29: "The Security Council also notes with serious concern that the Director General's report of 27 February 2006 (GOV/2006/15) lists a number of outstanding issues and concerns, including topics which could have a military nuclear dimension . . ."[27]

The stakes are clear and well understood worldwide as well. The Iranian nuclear program is dangerous enough in itself, but a likely consequence of an Iranian bomb is that other countries of the region would seek to acquire and deploy nuclear weapons. In addition, it would test the resilience of the nuclear nonproliferation regime. How much disorder can the regime absorb? Would it not be difficult for it to survive a second major blow, after North Korea's withdrawal from the NPT in January 2003? Finally, in light of the successful Iranian efforts to significantly increase the range of the Shehab-3 missile, potential targets might be hit far beyond the region in the future.

All the above notwithstanding, the result is more ambiguous concerning the level of international consensus to stop the Iranian nuclear ambitions. On one hand, when 27 out of 35 IAEA governors, including those representing the five permanent members of the UNSC plus major developing countries like Egypt, Brazil, and India, voted in favor of the resolution deciding to transfer the Iranian dossier to the UNSC in February 2006, the international consensus was greater than it had been only a few months earlier, in September 2005. On the other hand, it is remarkable that the consensus was reached on the basis that there would

---

26 "Implementation of the NPT Safeguards Agreement in the Islamic Republic of Iran," doc. no. GOV/2006/15, IAEA Board of Governors, February 27, 2006, http://www.iaea.org/Publications/Documents/Board/2006/gov2006-15.pdf.

27 "Security Council, in Presidential Statement, Underlines Importance of Iran's Re-establishing Full, Sustained Suspension of Uranium-Enrichment Activities," UNSC doc. no. SC/8679, March 29, 2006, www.un.org/News/Press/docs/2006/sc8679.doc.htm.

be no action whatsoever before March, a full month later, and that South Africa actually abstained (while Pretoria had previously indicated its intention to vote in favor of the draft text). The Arab world, which has had tense relations with Iran for a long time—many Arab countries backed Saddam Hussein in Iraq's 1980s war against Iran—also remains reluctant to speak out because of Israel. As recently as April 13, 2006, the first deputy premier and foreign minister of Qatar declared—in what can be considered to be a statement coming from the whole region—that the political pressure imposed on Iran should also be applied to Israel in order to rid the entire Middle East region of nuclear weapons.

In addition, the long discussion that took place in New York in March at the UNSC has clearly shown the lack of common strategy—even concerning the first step to adopt. This message was well received in Tehran. In some quarters, even after the June 2006 proposal by the Perm-5 and Germany, the belief still remains that another new and better offer to Iran would either produce a change of mind in Tehran or widen international support for sanctions. This belief reflects what is called the triumph of hope over experience. One needs only to look at the past three years to understand it.

To sum up, if the question to ask in the spring of 2006 is whether the four goals listed above have or have not been attained, the answer appears mixed at best.

Major Questions in May 2006

It is necessary to understand as much as possible some additional points:

What can reasonably be said concerning the status of the Iranian program in 2006? A number of hypotheses have been presented in the open literature and could be assessed. First, it now seems that most of the elements of a military program are in place, including the requirements for the reduction of UF6 to metal, the casting and machining of uranium metal into hemispherical forms, and the adaptation of the delivery vehicle to a nuclear warhead. Second, assuming that the first "significant quantity" (25 kilograms of HEU according to the IAEA) can be produced within a year by a 3,000 centrifuge pilot plant (of the P1 type), this plant—now that about 500 centrifuges have been assembled at the end of April—could be terminated as announced by

Tehran by the beginning of 2007 if the necessary components are available in Iran and the so-called SQ (significant quantity) could be produced as soon as 2007–08, assuming no serious technical problems.

In case more sophisticated centrifuges (of the P2 type) have been assembled as well in Iran, in some undisclosed location—as Mahmoud Ahmadinejad himself suggested in mid-April in a threatening statement—the possibility that Iran will soon be able to produce the adequate quantity of HEU would be even higher.[28] Designs for the P2 centrifuges were obtained in the 1990s from the A. Q. Khan clandestine network, and, according to Bukhary Syed Tahir, an important member of this network who was interrogated in Malaysia, three complete machines were acquired by Iran at about the same period. They may have been duplicated since then on a site not revealed to the IAEA inspectors and most probably under the control of the military. After having told Mohamed ElBaradei, the IAEA's director general, during his April visit to Tehran, that Iran would do its utmost to clarify the remaining outstanding issues,[29] Iranian authorities refused to answer questions about a second, secret, uranium-enrichment program—one of the most important pending questions.

To make a long story short, an Iranian nuclear bomb by 2008 is not an absurd hypothesis, taking into account progress made on issues other than the production of fissile material. What appears to be unrealistic is to suggest that at least five (or even ten) years are still needed to achieve this goal. After having overestimated the Iraqi capabilities in 2002 and 2003, we run the risk of underestimating the Iranian ones as the Iraqi capabilities were underestimated in 1990.

---

28 Mahmoud Ahmadinejad declared in April 2006 that the country was "presently conducting research" on the P2 centrifuges, highly efficient devices that he said could increase fourfold the amount of uranium the country is able to enrich: "Our centrifuges are the P1 type, and the next step is the P2, which has a capacity four times greater and on which we are presently conducting research."

29 The main questions are related to the P2 program, contamination with LEU and HEU, Iran's former dealings with A. Q. Khan, plutonium experiments, and suspected development of warheads. There was no attempt to answer any of the questions before April 28, when the IAEA director general was due to report on the implementation of the UNSC presidential statement. The IAEA report is clear on this point.

The milestone in Iran's program was reportedly passed on April 10—at the previously mentioned pilot centrifuge plant in Natanz—with the uranium enriched up to 3.5 percent. Gholam Reza Aghazadeh, the vice president and AEOI chief, asserted that this paved the way for "enrichment at an industrial scale," using the substantial UF6 feedstock gas already produced (more than 100 metric tons).

The announcement was intended to make three different points:

- Iran openly defied the UNSC's demand for the suspension of enrichment-related activities, reiterating that its nuclear program cannot be stopped.

- The nuclear enrichment technology was successfully mastered and the necessary demonstration had been done. The 164 centrifuges are not only assembled—as announced by mid-March—but actually working properly.

- The program is peaceful. Mahmoud Ahmadinejad immediately called again on foreign governments to "recognize and respect Iran's rights" and asked all nuclear officials in Iran "to speed up their work for the country's power stations."

To clarify the importance of the statement, the following comments may be useful:

- The technology needed to enrich uranium up to 3.5 percent or to weapons-grade level is essentially the same. In other words, if Iran masters uranium enrichment, it could enrich uranium to any level.

- The Iranian enriched uranium, even if the actual objective were to produce fuel for any power station, would not be compatible with the only existing Iranian nuclear power plant, Bushehr. Russian codes would be needed, and Russia has no intention of providing them.

- The Iranian program is progressing much faster than anticipated. It is more difficult to master R&D than to go from R&D to industrial scale. The call to speed up the work is a further indication of the Iranian plan. The point of self-sufficiency[30]—where Iran has the technical know-how and the capacity to build a bomb—is getting closer.

---

30 Already in May 2004, Ayatollah Ali Akbar Hashemi Rafsanjani declared, "That we are on the verge of nuclear breakout is true." (Islamic Republic News Agency [IRNA], May 25, 2004.)

- The presence of senior military commanders during the April 11 announcement underlined the true nature of the program. The armed forces chief of staff, General Hassan Firouzabadi, declared, "The West can do nothing and is obliged to extend to us the hand of friendship."

During his visit to Tehran on April 13, Mohamed ElBaradei, who expected "to convince Iran to take confidence-building measures including suspension of uranium enrichment activities until outstanding issues are clarified," met an even more defiant Iran than during previous meetings: "Today, Iran is a nuclear country and enjoys the position of a powerful country," and "there is no room for defeat or retreat." This attitude was confirmed again at the end of April after the IAEA report.

What is the position of the major actors in May 2006? Is it possible to recognize a (positive or negative) evolution of their positions? Are the major actors any closer to recognizing the implications (regional and global) of an Iranian bomb during the coming decade?

As stated above, the main problem here is not so much the recognition that an Iranian nuclear weapon would alter the Middle East — and beyond — in a significant way or that such a bomb would lead to further destabilization. There is a wide agreement concerning the possible effects of such a weapon in Saudi Arabia, Egypt, and Turkey, to name only three nations that could be tempted to reassess their nuclear abstention.

The main problem lies elsewhere, namely in the will to act to prevent this from happening. From this perspective, one should acknowledge that the Europeans at least made an attempt to find a solution.

Some contend that Russia did as well. Perhaps. But the Russian proposal has never appeared in any written form or shape, and no one seems to be in a position to describe it properly. The Trilateral Commission's authors of *Engaging with Russia: The Next Phase* (reporting at the Tokyo meeting) did hold extensive consultations in Moscow in mid-February 2006 at a time when the Iranian nuclear issue was high on the agenda. On this occasion, meetings were held with high-level government officials, including the foreign minister, the minister of atomic energy, and the secretary of the Security Council. Beyond Russia's concern that the United States was not more engaged than it had been at the inception of the conflict, all considered that there were no justifications for Iran possessing its own enrichment and reprocessing capabilities and that, if certain red lines were crossed by Iran, Russia would not stand by Iran as it does not want to be exposed to the world: "This red line is Iranian nuclear enrichment." A Russian official who has been even clearer on this point is Sergei Ivanov, and his position is that Russia will not allow any enrichment-related activity in Iran, including conversion.[31] After this red line was actually crossed for good in April 2006, however, Moscow did not adopt a firmer position.

In addition, by continuing to discuss the issue in Iran and in Russia, Moscow leaves the impression that the other players may not be informed about the whole story. More important, it creates doubts on what exactly its position is. The G-8 summit meeting in mid-July might be the decisive date. Meanwhile, centrifuges will continue to be assembled in Natanz.

Iran is raising a problem identified in the 1970s by Albert Wohlstetter, namely that the technologies for producing electricity and nuclear weapons (enrichment and reprocessing) are essentially the same. The key building blocks of a nuclear weapons program can be acquired if the declared use is for peaceful nuclear power. As Moscow well knows, the solution is to provide Iran with enrichment and spent-fuel removal services, particularly since indigenous enrichment is an order of magnitude more expensive than supply at market-based prices. But other issues may be at stake, particularly in the Caucasus and Central Asia—not to mention arms deals with Iran. Is Russia ready to accept Iran as a nuclear threshold nation? This is the question Russia—and China—should now answer.

Has the IAEA the necessary authority to verify, in a timely manner, the correctness and completeness of Iran's declarations? If not, can any institution other than the UNSC provide this necessary authority? The answer here is clear, and Pierre Goldschmidt, the former deputy director general for safeguards at the IAEA (now retired), has been a major asset in making the point: the IAEA needs additional authority to perform its task. Actually, the IAEA is in no position to impose prompt access to documents, individuals, and actual or suspected nuclear-related locations, even under the Additional Protocol. In its September 2, 2005, report, the IAEA director general, Mohamed ElBaradei, acknowledges this point: after three years of intrusive in-

---

31 Wehrkunde Security Conference, Munich, February 2006.

spections "the Agency is still not in a position to conclude that there are no undeclared nuclear materials and activities in Iran. The process of drawing such a conclusion, after an Additional Protocol is in force, under normal circumstances, is a time consuming process."[32]

What about the "exceptional circumstances," such as those prevailing in the Iranian case? As the February 2006 report states: "In the case of Iran, this conclusion can be expected to take even longer . . . because of the inadequacy of information available on its centrifuge enrichment program, the existence of a generic document related to the fabrication of nuclear weapons components, and the lack of clarification about the role of the military in Iran's nuclear program, including . . . about recent information available to the Agency concerning alleged weapon studies that could involve nuclear material."[33]

In the face of such a serious situation, the IAEA Board of Governors is equally limited in its capacity to impose more intrusive inspections because its resolutions do not provide the agency's inspectors with the necessary legal authority. Actually, only the UNSC can provide the IAEA with the necessary authority, and, in many respects, such would have been the best possible outcome of the first—March—debate in New York at the Security Council level.[34]

---

32 "Implementation of the NPT Safeguards Agreement in the Islamic Republic of Iran," doc. no. GOV/2005/67, IAEA Board of Governors, September 2, 2005, http://www.iaea.org/Publications/Documents/Board/2005/gov2005-67.pdf. In the April 28 IAEA report, the same assessment is repeated: "The Agency is unable to make progress in its efforts to provide assurance about the absence of undeclared nuclear material and activities in Iran." (See "Implementation of the NPT Safeguards Agreement in the Islamic Republic of Iran," doc. no. GOV/2006/27, IAEA Board of Governors, April 28, 2006, http://www.iaea.org/Publications/Documents/Board/2006/gov2006-27.pdf.) Such a conclusion justifies in itself the referral to the UNSC.

33 Reference may here be made to the so-called Green Salt Project. See "Implementation of the NPT Safeguards Agreement in the Islamic Republic of Iran," doc. no. GOV/2006/15, February 27, 2006, p. 8, paragraph 39.

34 In "The Urgent Need to Strengthen the Nuclear Non-Proliferation Regime," January 2006 (see http://www.comeclean.org.uk/articles.php?articleID=157), Pierre Goldschmidt suggests "urgent action" by the UNSC to adopt a "generic binding resolution that would

(Continued on next page)

Unfortunately, not a single word can be found concerning additional authority for the IAEA inspectors in the weak presidential statement that was adopted on March 29, 2006,[35] although the reference to the first operative paragraph of the February 27, 2006, IAEA resolution in this statement can be interpreted as an indirect mention of this issue because it requires "access to individuals, documentation relating to procurement, dual use equipment, certain military owned workshops and research and development." But, again, the IAEA Board of Governors resolutions do not provide the necessary authority, and if the wish is to strengthen the inspectors' legal authority, the UNSC would need to adopt a much more explicit position on the subject.

The March opportunity having been lost, the chance for the Security Council to impose intrusive verification measures, in order, inter alia, to locate undisclosed sites and to inspect them, appears slim. This is true even though Mahmoud Ahmadinejad's statement concerning active research on P2 type centrifuges would be an excellent reason to adopt such a policy in order to restore IAEA's credibility.

Is the Security Council ready to raise the diplomatic stakes? By deceiving the IAEA about its nuclear activities, Iran has given up whatever rights it once enjoyed under the NPT. And according to IAEA statute, noncompliance must be reported to the Security Council. After more than two years of "suspension" for such reporting, justified by the ongoing negotiations with the Europeans, the long-standing threat was carried out in February, and the UNSC adopted a first action—the March 29 presidential statement—at the UNSC at the end of March.

The text was so weak, however, that it was almost self-defeating.[36] Produced in three weeks after much debate in New York, it was re-

---

(*Note 34 continued from preceding page*) establish three peaceful measures for containing crises when a state is found by the IAEA to be in noncompliance with its safeguards obligations." These measures are "strengthening the IAEA's authority to conduct the inspections necessary to resolve uncertainties, deterring the noncompliant state from thinking it could withdraw from the NPT and enjoy the benefits of ill-gotten material and equipment, and suspending fuel cycle–related activities in the state." The wise advice was not followed by corresponding action.

35 See text in Appendix to this chapter.

36 Most diplomats would argue that the major weakness was not the content of the statement but the time needed to reach agreement on it.

jected in less than one hour by Tehran. Iran furthermore announced in April that it would accelerate the pace of its nuclear program. After the April 28 IAEA report to the Security Council, where no progress at all can be observed and some deterioration has even been noted,[37] the responsibility of the UN body has only increased. Some commentators underline the weakening of the Security Council if it proves unable to address the issue in a satisfactory fashion. As of June 2006, the picture is bleak in this respect.

The North Korean case has already illustrated this point. Since January 2003, after Pyongyang's withdrawal — the first ever — from the NPT, the UNSC has been unable to produce even a presidential statement, mainly because of Chinese obstruction. Such is not exactly the situation today with Iran, but the presidential statement adopted in March was a political gesture carrying no legal obligation, and further steps are still in limbo. In short, there is no strategy, not even to make the suspension mandatory under Chapter VII of the charter.[38] Russia and China essentially want the Iranian dossier to come back to the IAEA, a technical institution that does not even benefit from additional powers since the UNSC March debate.[39] This may have significant implications, including beyond the Iranian case.

If the UNSC is no longer considered efficient enough to perform its responsibility in dealing with noncompliance of major international treaties, we risk returning to the powerlessness of the League of Na-

---

37 In fact, the situation has worsened. The IAEA notes the statements made by high-level Iranian officials concerning R&D and testing of P2 centrifuges that it has asked Iran to clarify without any success so far. In another area — plutonium experiments — the assessment of the IAEA is more worrisome than in previous reports (see page 5, paragraph 17, of "Implementation of the NPT Safeguards Agreement in the Islamic Republic of Iran," doc. no. GOV/2006/27, April 28, 2006, http:// www.iaea.org/Publications/Documents/Board/2006/gov2006-27.pdf).

38 Initially, the Europeans were seeking a quick presidential statement (during the first week), leaving Tehran only 15 days to comply. This first step having not succeeded, the following stages — a resolution under Chapter VII — will be much harder.

39 Interestingly enough, such is also the Iranian objective. On April 2, the Iranian ambassador to the IAEA, Aliasghar Soldaniyeh, declared in an interview on CNN that "the best option for the Security Council is doing nothing and leave the IAEA complete its work," and on April 29, Iran said it would allow inspections if the UNSC drops the case.

tions. Other leaders risk declaring, after Mahmoud Ahmadinejad, "We do not give a damn about such resolutions." And this defiance would take place at the worst possible moment, after the failed 2005 NPT review conference heightens the risk of truly unraveling the entire international nonproliferation regime so painstakingly set up over the last decades, and at a time when violence is on the rise worldwide.

Concluding Remarks

Iran is located in a very sensitive zone that has seen four wars in the past two decades, and an Iranian nuclear bomb would be a further destabilizing factor. There is little doubt on this point. In May 2006, the Iranian nuclear issue reached a turning point, particularly after April 11, 2006, and the subsequent statement concerning the P2 research program. Both announcements have sounded alarm bells the world over. In addition, new satellite imagery indicated in April 2006 that Iran had expanded its uranium enrichment conversion site at Isfahan and reinforced its Natanz underground uranium enrichment plant.

Reconciliatory efforts with Iran have met little success since 2003 and are unlikely to be more successful with the expansive and defiant mood of the current Iranian president. The Security Council, in a March presidential statement, underlined the importance of Iran's reestablishing full and sustained suspension of uranium enrichment-related activities, called on Iran to take steps required by the IAEA Board of Governors, and requested a report from the IAEA director general in 30 days.

The demand fell on deaf ears with President Ahmadinejad and Ayatollah Khamenei, both of whom said that their country's atomic ambitions were not open to negotiation. Far from acceding to the UNSC demands, they announced the decision to accelerate their program. To complete an already dark picture, Iran's supreme leader added insult to injury by declaring on April 25 that Iran was ready to share its nuclear technology with other countries: "The Islamic Republic of Iran is prepared to transfer the experience, knowledge and technology of its scientists."[40] This is pretty close to what Kim Jong-Il has said in similar circumstances.

---

40 Supreme Leader Ayatollah Ali Khamenei, at a meeting with President Omar al-Bashir of Sudan in Tehran, April 25, 2006; reported by IRNA.

At this stage, despite all of the above—and in particular the complete disregard by Tehran of the UNSC's authority—there is no political consensus for imposing sanctions. The only chance of stopping Iranian nuclear ambitions diplomatically is not another negotiation with Tehran. This would only allow Iran to gain more time. The only chance to achieve it, by significantly raising the cost of Iranian defiance, is still not attracting the necessary support. There is even less consensus about using force against Tehran. And, finally, there is no indication that the major powers will demonstrate their ability to balance their domestic interests with their global responsibilities. Meanwhile, the Iranian nuclear program is progressing more rapidly than anticipated in Natanz. And Tehran shows it has learned from Pyongyang that brinkmanship brings rewards.[41]

The disconnection between the pace of diplomacy and the pace of the Iranian nuclear military program could eventually produce the worst possible outcome: either a nuclear Iran, with other nations following suit in the neighborhood, or another military action in the Middle East, with unpredictable consequences in the region and beyond.[42]

The combination of Ahmadinejad's inflammatory rhetoric, the progress Iran has made in assembling its centrifuges, and the difficult March discussion at the UNSC has increased interest in evaluating the military option. Contrary to many claims, a military attack is not "unconceivable,"[43] although it would necessitate sustainable attacks on

---

41 North Korea is taking great advantage of the Iranian crisis that attracts international attention for Tehran while Pyongyang is progressing on its nuclear program as well. Tokyo may be the place where this development is followed with most anxiety.

42 Iran may be wrong in counting on U.S. distraction (Iraq, Afghanistan, energy prices, and midterm elections). The administration may come to share the view recently expressed by Senator John McCain (R-Ariz.): "In the end, there is only one thing worse than military action, and that is a nuclear armed Iran."

43 It is interesting to recall, as Edward Luttwak does in a May 2006 piece published by *Commentary* ("Three Reasons Not to Bomb Iran—Yet"), that the last time the United States seriously considered the use of force in Iran, much larger operations were envisaged. It was in 1978, to defend the country from a Soviet thrust to the Persian Gulf, "a complete light infantry division would have been needed just as an advance guard to screen the build-up of the main forces."

a relatively large number of targets that are well-defended, passively and actively.[44]

In June 2006, after the IAEA report to the UNSC, the UNSC presidential statement, and the Perm-5 + 1 offer to Tehran, all options remain open in an attempt to resolve the crisis. President Bush himself declared that "diplomacy is just beginning." But if diplomacy does not produce better and quicker results in the months to come, what is now in no way inevitable might become increasingly likely, possibly after the November elections in the United States: a series of conventional air strikes against nuclear and ballistic missile plants in Iran. If such is the outcome, it would be the result of a complete mismanagement of the diplomatic process because there was enough leverage—and enough time—to reach different results. And those who now worry so much about oil prices and instability in the Middle East should think about the effect of an Iranian nuclear bomb on both issues.

Appendix

Statement by the President of the UN Security Council, March 29, 2006

At the 5403rd meeting of the Security Council, held on 29 March 2006, in connection with the Council's consideration of the item entitled "Nonproliferation," the President of the Security Council made the following statement on behalf of the Council:

"The Security Council reaffirms its commitment to the Treaty on the Non-proliferation of Nuclear Weapons and recalls the right of States Party, in conformity with Articles I and II of that Treaty, to develop research, production and use of nuclear energy for peaceful purposes without discrimination.

The Security Council notes with serious concern the many IAEA reports and resolutions related to Iran's nuclear programme, reported to it by the IAEA Director General, including the February IAEA Board Resolution (GOV/2006/14).

---

44 In addition to the military cost of action, there would also be a domestic cost to take into account.

The Security Council also notes with serious concern that the Director General's report of 27 February 2006 (GOV/2006/15) lists a number of outstanding issues and concerns, including topics which could have a military nuclear dimension, and that the IAEA is unable to conclude that there are no undeclared nuclear materials or activities in Iran.

The Security Council notes with serious concern Iran's decision to resume enrichment-related activities, including research and development, and to suspend cooperation with the IAEA under the Additional Protocol.

The Security Council calls upon Iran to take the steps required by the IAEA Board of Governors, notably in the first operative paragraph of its resolution GOV/2006/14, which are essential to build confidence in the exclusively peaceful purpose of its nuclear programme and to resolve outstanding questions, and underlines, in this regard, the particular importance of re-establishing full and sustained suspension of all enrichment-related and reprocessing activities, including research and development, to be verified by the IAEA.

The Security Council expresses the conviction that such suspension and full, verified Iranian compliance with the requirements set out by the IAEA Board of Governors would contribute to a diplomatic, negotiated solution that guarantees Iran's nuclear programme is for exclusively peaceful purposes, and underlines the willingness of the international community to work positively for such a solution which will also benefit nuclear non-proliferation elsewhere.

The Security Council strongly supports the role of the IAEA Board of Governors and commends and encourages the Director General of the IAEA and its secretariat for their ongoing professional and impartial efforts to resolve outstanding issues in Iran, and underlines the necessity of the IAEA continuing its work to clarify all outstanding issues relating to Iran's nuclear programme.

The Security Council requests in 30 days a report from the Director General of the IAEA on the process of Iranian compliance with the steps required by the IAEA Board, to the IAEA Board of Governors and in parallel to the Security Council for its consideration."

4

East Asia and Weapons of Mass Destruction in North Korea: Strategic Drivers, Future Paths, and Nonproliferation Dynamics

Chung Min Lee

Asia is not only the new epicenter of global politics and economics, it is also home to or the intersecting point of the world's greatest powers and the most pressing nuclear-prone subzones stretching across the vast Asian landmass. No other region in the world today or in the foreseeable future confronts such a vast array of security challenges: three of the world's seven declared nuclear states are Asian (China, India, and Pakistan); five out of the top ten largest standing armies are Asian (China, India, North Korea, South Korea, and Pakistan); and the most dangerous nuclear breakout states—North Korea and Iran—are Asian.

For more than a half century, Asia has also been home to key geopolitical hot spots: the Korean peninsula, the Taiwan Strait, and Kashmir in South Asia. Beyond these more well-known hazards, Asia also confronts the specter of a growing cluster of failing or failed states that could result in significant human security casualties. More worrisome, however, is the potential for sustained political instability in two key candidate states—North Korea and Pakistan—that could impinge upon their respective abilities to ensure integrity over their weapons of mass destruction (WMD) or nuclear forces or facilities.

While the possibility of a full-scale conventional war has decreased substantially since the end of the Cold War, the uses of force as vital instruments of state policy or, at a minimum, as capabilities-based assurances remain very much alive in Asia's strategically consequential states. In brief, discontinuities and disequilibrium stemming from any one of the threats mentioned above would have global repercussions based on Asia's increasing share of global wealth and productivity. Thus, proliferation dynamics in Asia and attendant consequences are systemic and global even as their origins are regional and national. In turn, this dichotomy imposes key policy constraints on all of the principal actors for conventional behavioral norms and regularized state actions have been, and may well continue to be, insufficient.

Such a stark security snapshot stands in sharp contrast to the region's robust economic and commercial picture. But this bifurcated and increasingly intertwined security and economic complex encapsulates the Asian dilemma of the early twenty-first century: Are Asia's central security dilemmas just beginning? Or can they be mitigated, if not prevented, by greater economic integration, political transparency and democratization, and formalization of confidence-building regimes? For the policy maker and strategist alike, both characterizations are equally correct but also insufficient: correct in the sense that Asia rightly features integrative and disintegrative forces, but insufficient since such appraisals do not provide for potential paradigm shifts in the Asian conception and actualization of security choices.

This essay attempts to offer a partial, and limited, perspective on seeing the Asian WMD phenomenon as a chain of interrelated but also separate and unique political conditions that don't necessarily fit in with more conventional arms control or even nonproliferation norms and strategies. Specifically, this essay has three main objectives. First, to assess the viability of the increasingly popular proposition that market-driven conceptions of security—the growing delegitimization of military precepts of security—hold true in the emerging East Asia. Second, to delineate key quandaries and tipping points in the context of WMD in two key subregions—South Asia and Northeast Asia—and the possible triggers that could severely impair prospects for stability. And, third, brief WMD profiles of the four main actors in the Asian WMD picture—China, India, Pakistan, and North Korea—with national policy ramifications and strategic lessons that may obviate partially or at the very least lessen marginally the excessive and unprecedented security dichotomies confronting Asia.

Twin Faces of East Asian Security

In April 1975, the fall of South Vietnam, Cambodia, and Laos seemed to confirm the much-debated domino theory in East Asia. An Asian arc of socialism now stretched from the Russian Far East over North Korea, China, and Southeast Asia. Although key components of U.S. grand strategy in the postwar era remained valid—the reconstruction of Western Europe and Japan and the forging of a web of U.S.-led security alliances—many wondered if the U.S. strategy of containment would henceforth be outflanked or undercut.[1] By 2005, however, or merely three decades after the apogee of communism in East Asia, traces of 1975 were nearly invisible. With the notable exception of North Korea, all of the constituent states of the Asian arc of socialism rejected in practice, if not in theory, centralized economic planning and have embraced, to varying degrees, market-driven liberalization. In hindsight, 1975 was a tipping point year not because of the success of communism but rather as the beginning of the end of orthodox communism in the most important, powerful, and transformative member of the Asian arc of socialism, the People's Republic of China (PRC).

The Primacy of Market-Driven Security?

China's eventual embracement of unprecedented economic reforms would unleash forces that were impossible to harness and refine under orthodox communism: the ability to compete, if not surpass, the more developed and, critically important, more powerful Western states. As Henry Kissinger noted in 2005, the center of gravity in world affairs is shifting from the Atlantic to Asia and "the most rapidly developing countries are located in Asia, with a growing means to vindicate their perception of the national interest."[2] Others have asserted that the center of the new power arrangement in Asia is unlikely to be led by Japan, but rather by China and eventually India.[3] Commensurate with Asia's rise, many have argued that a fundamental rethinking of the Cold War security template was in the making; henceforth, the primacy of the market would surpass endemic political struggles within Asia.

It is true that consonant with the absence of major interstate wars in Asia since the unification of Vietnam in 1975, the acceleration of unprecedented economic growth, and the concomitant flourishing of

1 James Kurth, "Global Threats and American Strategies: From Communism in 1955 to Islamism in 2005," *Orbis* (Fall 2005), 638.

2 Henry Kissinger, "China Shifts Centre of Gravity," *The Australian,* June 13, 2005, www.taiwansecurity.org/News?2005/AS-130605.htm.

3 James F. Hoge Jr., "A Global Power Shift in the Making" *Foreign Affairs,* (July/August 2004).

democracy since the late 1980s, wars as instruments of state policy seem to have lost much of their potency.[4] Although democratic peace theory offers one partial answer to the waning of interstate wars in Asia, it can't be construed as a sufficient condition given outstanding democracy deficits in the region. A more compelling reason perhaps can be traced to a corollary to the democratic peace theory: namely, that fully marketized economies as well as transition economies have far more to gain from mitigating complex crises and conflicts rather than building up military capital. It goes without saying that the dissolution of the Soviet Union and the global ending of the Cold War diluted contestations of ideology with the exception of the two Koreas and the cross-strait relationship.

One of the most positive attributes of the Asian security triangle is also the most visible: unparalleled economic growth and political transformations. In 2004, the JACIKs (Japan, ASEAN, China, India, and Korea) accounted for 23 percent of global GDP—making them the third economic hub of the world together with the EU (30 percent) and the United States (28 percent). In terms of merchandise trade, the JACIKs accounted for 25 percent of global exports compared with nearly 37 percent for the European economies. If we assume that the broadening of economic globalization will continue, then East Asia stands to be a key driver and beneficiary of globalization. Security at this level is mostly conceived and understood in the context of a series of increasingly pervasive economic and trade linkages to sustain, augment, and deepen domestic growth rates. Notwithstanding the prevalence of vexing political and historical disputes, the prevention of wide-ranging and prolonged economic dislocation (such as the 1997 Asian financial crisis) is the prima facie security objective at this tier. This is also the most public face of East Asia.

---

4 This is not to suggest that East Asia has been devoid of conflicts since that time. The 1979 border war between China and Vietnam and the 1999 Kargil conflict between India and Pakistan are just two examples of low-intensity conflicts. Conflicts, genocides, and suppressions within states persisted for much of the 1970s and 1980s: the Khmer Rouge's killing fields in Cambodia, the subsequent civil war instigated by Vietnam's invasion of Cambodia, the Kwangju incident of May 1980, and the June 1989 crackdown in Tiananmen. Notwithstanding these atrocities, however, no two states in East Asia have engaged in full-scale war since the conclusion of the Vietnamese War in 1975.

The cumulative and relentless rise of East Asia over the past three decades has been heralded as the coming of age of the Pacific Era. Three of the world's most populous states are in the greater Asia region: China, India, and Indonesia. The UN estimates that by 2025, India's population will reach 1.4 billion or the same level as China's, whereas by 2050 its population is expected to grow to 1.6 billion compared with China's population, which is expected to fall below 1.4 billion.[5] Measured by sustained economic growth since the 1970s (with notable dips during the oil crises of the early 1970s and the Asian financial crisis of 1997–98), East Asia's comprehensive growth has been spurred by the absence of major interstate wars since the end of the Vietnam conflict in 1975.

Thus, if current trends continue, the rise of new great powers, chief among them China and India, is likely to parallel the advent of unified Germany in the nineteenth century and the United States in the early twentieth century with similar global ramifications.[6] Although the future trajectories of China and India cannot but confront a series of nonlinear hiccups, one forecast predicts that by 2025 the BRIC (Brazil, Russia, India, and China) economies together could account for 50 percent of the Group of Six economies, or an increase of 35 percent from current levels.[7] The same report postulates that by 2050 only the United States and Japan may still be among the six largest economies.[8]

As the Bush administration prepared to enter the White House in January 2001, significant attention was attached to the cumulative rise of China and what this portended for U.S. grand strategy well into the twenty-first century. A decade after the dissolution of the former Soviet Union and a wholesale redrawing of the global strategic template—exemplified most tellingly by German unification and the emergence of new strategic enclaves such as Central Asia—security planners in the United States were continuing to search for a viable, sustainable, and politically marketable post-Soviet doctrine.

---

5 For additional information on global and regional population projections, see *World Population Prospects: The 2004 Revision* (New York: United Nations, February 2005).

6 *Mapping the Future: Report of the National Intelligence Council's 2020 Project* (Washington, D.C.: National Intelligence Council, December 2004), 9.

7 Dominic Wilson and Roopa Purushothaman, "Dreaming with BRICs: The Path to 2050," Goldman Sachs Global Economics Paper no. 99, (October 1, 2003), 4.

8 Ibid.

Pigeonholing China as a catchall threat reminiscent of the Cold War era posed significant problems and drawbacks. Consonant with China's unprecedented economic growth since the late 1980s and the growing attractiveness of the world's largest consumer market, it was becoming increasingly difficult to argue that China was at once the biggest boon to U.S. and Western business interests while at the very same time the most logical threat-in-waiting. Equally problematic was the lack of consensus among U.S. allies (in Asia but also in Europe) that China was a credible security threat requiring a more proactive, "virtual containment" policy vis-à-vis the People's Republic of China. Yet, unlike the Soviet Union, which was not a magnet or a driver of the global economy, China cannot be pegged into any one box. One seasoned observer has written:

> China has always presented a great conundrum for the United States. It is the kind of power Washington deals with the least well: a nation that is neither clearly friend nor clearly foe, simultaneously a strategic threat and a critical trade and investment partner . . . The future of the relationship depends on how Chinese politics evolve: whether China provokes a showdown with Taiwan and uses its economic might to achieve Asian hegemony, or develops into an increasingly pluralistic society in which economic interests dictate continuing good relations with its neighbors.[9]

The China Conundrum and Asian Choices

The catastrophic events of September 11, 2001, from a U.S. perspective resulted in a strategic about-face: the full wrath of the United States was henceforth to be directed against Al Qaeda, its allies, and its strategic partners (for example, Jamal Islamiyah). While China continued to solicit attention, the global war against terrorism was now not only the newest war but also the most important one. And yet, while the zealous environment-shaping ethos of the neoconservatives faced increasing hurdles and setbacks, their initial focus on China was not entirely wrong.

---

9 Francis Fukuyama, "Re-Envisioning Asia," *Foreign Affairs* (January/February 2005), www.foreignaffairs.org/2005101faessay84107/francis-fukuyama/re-envisioning-asia.

Although a lively debate continues about whether China is set to become the next theater peer that could fundamentally challenge U.S. supremacy by 2020–30 or so, there is little doubt that Chinese power is going to become one of the most important strategic drivers in East Asia in the first half of the twenty-first century. Notwithstanding the shock with which 9/11 was perceived throughout the world, including East Asia, the global war against terrorism "has had a fairly strong albeit temporary impact on the trends of globalization, regionalization, and balance of power politics in East Asia."[10] To reiterate, while the neoconservatives' embrace of the China threat is replete with significant inconsistencies, virtually every facet of East Asia's security today has a Chinese imprint. How key players in the region—individually, collectively, or in consort with the United States—cope with China's cumulative rise as they implement their respective national strategies is going to become a central determinant of East Asia's twenty-first century geostrategic template.

This does not mean, however, that China is going to displace the United States as the principal guarantor of East Asian security any time in the near future. As one succinct China watcher has commented, "It is tempting—but premature—to conclude that the Asian regional system has become Sinocentric or dominated by China . . . The United States remains the region's most powerful actor, although its power and influence are neither unconstrained nor uncontested."[11]

Despite China's increasingly robust defense modernization as evinced by an average 11 percent growth per annum since 1997 and selectively ambitious power projection capabilities, most analysts believe that the preponderance of U.S. military power means that China is unlikely to become a peer competitor of the United States. For it to do so, China would have to "close the gap with the U.S. military, create power projection capabilities that would threaten the American position in East Asia, and replace the former Soviet Union as a global secu-

---

10 Lowell Dittmer, "East Asia in the 'New Era,' in World Politics," World Politics 5 (October 2002), 65. Dittmer goes on to note that "the 'war' cannot in my view really be said to have initiated a new era in world politics, at least as perceived from East Asia."

11 David Shambaugh, "China Engages Asia: Reshaping the Regional Order," *International Security* 29, no. 3 (Winter 2004/05): 66.

rity threat."[12] Notwithstanding these caveats, however, China is bound to concentrate on retaining requisite military capabilities that would allow it to dominate over most regional actors as a near competitor of other great powers, notably Russia, Japan, and even perhaps a unified Korea in addition to "developing politically useful capabilities to punish American forces if they were to intervene in a conflict of great interest to China."[13]

Thus, to the extent that China has all of the requisite conditions in becoming a regional peer, the prevailing post–World War II status quo anchored in the form of the U.S.-Japan alliance is going to come under increasing threat. Even if China is unable to field power projection platforms that could directly contest U.S. military supremacy in East Asia, no other power has the economic, political, and selective military capabilities that could hamper, if not undermine, U.S. and allied interests in the region. China's imports from the region since the late 1990s have increased sharply, at an annualized rate of over 30 percent, to $369 billion in 2004.[14] If China is able to sustain its military modernization drive based on fairly robust economic growth, it stands to reason that a growing cluster of Asian states (for example, ASEAN members) may opt to generate simultaneous benefits by playing off China and the U.S.-Japan alliance. But such moves, if realized, could pose more risks than benefits since, at the very least, China would require de facto political obeisance with zero tolerance for any direct or even indirect support in the event of a critical flare-up in the Taiwan Strait.[15]

Asian Insecurities, Hybrid Conflicts, and WMD

Describing, much less forecasting, Asian security complexes is a focal point of academic and policy debate. Barry Buzan, for example, has

12 Thomas J. Christensen, "Posing Problems without Catching Up: China's Rise and Challenges for U.S. Security Policy," *International Security* 25, no. 4 (Spring 2001): 8.

13 Ibid.

14 Christopher Wood and Joe Man, "The Earth Moves: China Flexes its Military Muscle," CLSA Asia-Pacific Markets, March 2005, 4–5.

15 For a discussion on Chinese forays into Southeast Asia and attendant responses, see Dana Dillon and John J. Tkacik Jr., "China's Quest for Asia," *Policy Review* 134 (December 2005–January 2006), www.policyreview.org/134/dillon.html.

argued that post–Cold War East Asia is likely to sway between "mild conflict formation" and a "rather odd and weak sort of security regime" where an outside power, the United States, continues to play a critical role.[16] Aaron Friedberg asserted in 1994 that a rising Asia was essentially "ripe for rivalry," given the dearth of functioning multilateral security mechanisms to mitigate deeply entrenched security problems.[17] Counterarguments and intermediate assertions have been made in the interim, ranging from a return to some form of an intrinsically Asian hierarchical order to more nuanced attention to "shared regional norms, rising economic interdependence, and institutional linkages."[18] Still others such as Kent Calder have asserted that the paradox of East Asia, and Northeast Asia in particular, is that for a region with the world's highest concentration of great powers or "the most purposive and strategic nations on earth," only limited progress has been made in confronting, even perceiving, common economic development and security problems.[19] He proposes, among other solutions, the need to foster greater critical juncture mechanisms or cajole collective action by incrementally reducing barriers.

Contending schools of thought on East Asia's security futures can be broken down into three basic groups:

- The realist and the neorealist school that places importance on power distributions and countering a range of threats through deterrence, balancing, and use of force;

- The institutional and multilateralist school that emphasizes norm creation and building through regimes and institutions in order to alleviate acute security challenges through mutually reinforcing behavioral change; and

---

16 For details, see Barry Buzan, "Security Architecture in Asia: The Interplay of Regional and Global Levels," *Pacific Review* 16, no. 2 (2003): 143–173.

17 See Aaron Friedberg, "Ripe for Rivalry: Prospects for Peace in Multipolar Asia," *International Security* 18, no. 3 (Winter 1993/94): 5-33.

18 Amitav Acharya, "Will Asia's Past Be Its Future?," *International Security* 28, no. 3 (Winter 2003/04): 151–153.

19 Kent Calder and Min Ye, "Regionalism and Critical Junctures: Explaining the 'Organization Gap' in Northeast Asia," *Journal of East Asian Studies* 4 (2004): 219.

- The constructivist school that seeks to understand entrenched conceptions of security and insecurity through a thorough vetting of domestic determinants and ideational precepts to find more common security denominators.

What poses particular problems for the policy maker vis-à-vis East Asia is that at different levels or tiers in the Asian security puzzle, all three elements are evident.

Thus, the Asian security complex of the early twenty-first century can perhaps be best described as a brittle triangle—at once exhibiting all three elements noted above and imbued with a series of geostrategic fault lines that could result in pockets and streams of severe disequilibrium.[20] Although this essay focuses on the WMD phenomenon in East Asia, including the Chinese, Indo-Pakistani, and North Korean cases, nuclear futures in Asia are likely to be driven by a confluence of forces—political, ideological, military, and technological—that are far more complex and riskier than those that affected the U.S.-Soviet nuclear competition during the Cold War. That the United States and the USSR in consort with the other declared nuclear powers successfully averted global Armageddon is to be applauded, but it still provides limited comfort in the context of Asia's emergent nuclear quagmire.

This is not to suggest that Asia is on the brink of or is inexorably marching along the path to nuclear perdition. Indeed, if the analogy of the brittle triangle is valid, increasingly pervasive trade and economic linkages may well serve to mitigate outstanding political disputes or, at a minimum, restrain more acute responses. Although neither the South Asian Association of Regional Cooperation (SAARC) or the wider ASEAN Regional Forum (ARF) is likely to have much impact on hard security issues, they could serve to alleviate tensions at the margins.[21] Finally, the drive toward greater economic integration and, equally important, political stability and security, which are key prerequisites for sustained growth, serves as a key incentive in deescalating major security challenges before they cross the bridge of no return.

---

20 Asia in this essay is used to refer to the so-called JACIK states: Japan, ASEAN, China, India, and Korea. Given the prominence of Pakistan in the regional WMD equation, Pakistan is also considered a part of the JACIK grouping. Of course, subregional classifications—South Asia (India and Pakistan), Southeast Asia (ASEAN plus Australia), and Northeast Asia (China, Japan, and the two Koreas)—are used throughout the essay for differentiation purposes.

Asia and WMD: Key Issues

The principal states of concern or, more bluntly put, "rogues with nuclear weapons"—Iran and North Korea—lie at critical geopolitical fault lines along the Eurasian landmass. The three declared Asian nuclear powers—China, India, and Pakistan—also figure prominently in these fault lines that have been home to Asia's most vicious wars after World War II: the three Indo-Pakistani wars since 1948, the Korean War from 1950 to 1953, the Vietnamese conflict from 1954 to 1975, and the Iran-Iraq War of 1980–88. While the propensity for war has declined measurably since the end of the Cold War, all three subregions confront undercurrents or political turbidities that could disrupt stability in and around their subregions.

The impact of cascading crises in the event of Iranian and North Korean breakouts is difficult to map out although it is not unreasonable to assume that it is bound to trigger a range of counterresponses with potentially devastating consequences. Although other regional states have attempted to pursue indigenous nuclear weapons programs—South Korea and Taiwan in the 1970s—they were scuttled early on under intense pressure from the United States. In South Korea's case, it is widely believed that Seoul began a nuclear research program in the early 1970s following the withdrawal of the U.S. Seventh Division pursuant to the Nixon Doctrine. By 1975, however, the United States pressured France into stopping delivery of a planned reprocessing facility that ended, for all practical purposes, South Korea's initial forays into nuclear weapons research by January 1976.[22]

To date, there is no evidence that either South Korea or Taiwan is currently undertaking clandestine nuclear weapons programs although South Korea reported to the International Atomic Energy Agency (IAEA) in August 2004 that South Korea had conducted experiments

---

21 Although multilateral gatherings such as the SAARC summits are notorious for seemingly superfluous statements of intent, it is worth noting that key transnational issues such as terrorism, the security of small states, and depoliticizing key emergent problems are being considered as critical agendas. See "Dhaka Declaration," Thirteenth SAARC Summit, Dhaka, November 13, 2005, http://www.saarc-sec.org/main.php.

22 Junkman Kang and H. A. Eielson, "South Korea's Shifting and Controversial Interest in Spent Fuel Reprocessing," *Nonproliferation Review* (Spring 2001).

to enrich a very small amount of uranium—0.2 grams—through atomic vapor laser isotope separation (AVLIS) as well as plutonium separation in 2000.[23] Subsequently, the IAEA dispatched an inspection team to South Korea in September and on November 11, 2004, issued a report on implementation of nuclear safeguards in South Korea, including that the Republic of Korea (ROK) had taken corrective actions.

For its part, while Japan has steadfastly maintained its nonnuclear principles since the end of World War II, it currently possesses more than 45,000 kilograms of MOX fuel (from excess plutonium) although opposition from environmental groups, among others, has pressured the Japanese government into pursuing its MOX fuel program much more slowly than originally planned. Coupled with an increasingly robust civilian space program, including long-range launch vehicles such as the new and modified M-5 and the H-2, many experts believe that Japan has all of the requisite technology to cross the threshold in a relatively short time. Both South Korea and Taiwan also have extensive civilian nuclear facilities given their high dependence on nuclear-generated power. Depending on a range of future scenarios, Seoul and Taipei could also opt for a nuclear option although such moves would result in severe consequences in their respective security ties with the United States.

Against this backdrop lies the PRC. Until the rapprochement between Beijing and Moscow in the late 1980s, Chinese nuclear policy was geared to satisfy four main goals: homeland defense in case of a protracted Sino-Soviet conflict, given the wide-ranging disparities between the People's Liberation Army (PLA) and the Soviet armed forces situated along the border at that time; countering U.S. strategic footprints in East Asia; augmenting frontier defense in lieu of China's long-standing competition with India and, in the process, bolstering Pakistani defenses as a key strategic buffer; and applying sustained pressure on the authorities in Taiwan. Minus the drawdown in Chinese forces along the Sino-Russian border and a recalibrated relationship with Russia, China's nuclear policy remains relatively unchanged with the caveat that it now enjoys significantly upgraded power projection capabilities. The PLA has continued to emphasize strategic nuclear

---

23 Daniel A. Pinkston, "South Korea's Nuclear Experiments," CNS research story, November 9, 2004, http://www.cns.miis.edu/pubs/week/ 041109.htm.

modernization, particularly in sea-based platforms (SLBMs) and inter-continental ballistic missiles (ICBMs).

What many analysts miss, however, is China's own role in the now defunct A. Q. Khan network. China provided long-term assistance for Pakistan's nuclear weapons programs in addition to supplying North Korea with a range of surface-to-air missiles. The great Pakistani-North Korean swap — nuclear technologies for ballistic missiles — was a match made in heaven. The Silk Road thus dangerously became the WMD Road with consequences that have yet to be fully played out.

WMD Tipping Points and Quandaries

What then, are the key asymmetrical tipping points and quandaries that could significantly alter the geostrategic balance in the respective subregions? There are four predicaments with a range of triggers that may result in a series of cascading, complex crises. All of them are not inevitable, but conditions for stability require gargantuan and coordinated political, economic, and military efforts. Akin to a seiche or an underwater wave that does not surface but can have devastating impacts all the same, some of the tremors that could adversely affect these fault lines may have relatively long life cycles that will only surface after coming into contact with other extraneous forces.[24] In other words, more viable nonproliferation mechanisms must always be excavated but, in the end, they may be largely inefficient because their targets are fixed on visible and more tangible outputs. Seen from this perspective, the following quandaries deserve closer examination in the context of East Asian WMD.

Interplay between failing states, WMD, and the stability-instability paradox. Throughout the so-called first nuclear era (1945–91),[25]

---

24 For a cogent assessment of the current and emerging surface issues in Northeast Asia, see International Crisis Group, "Northeast Asia's Undercurrents of Conflict," Asia Report no. 108, December 15, 2005, http://www.crisisgroup.org/library/documents/asia/ 108_north_east_asia_s_undercurrents_of_conflict.pdf. The report focuses on three clusters of conflict undercurrents in this region: territorial disputes, clashing perceptions of history, and rising nationalism.

25 See Paul Bracken, "The Second Nuclear Age," *Foreign Affairs* 79 (January/February 2000). According to Bracken, "The rise of Asian

(Continued on next page)

the only declared nuclear weapon state that faced sustained political volatility was the PRC during the interregnum between the disastrous Great Leap Forward and the Cultural Revolution. Even so, the political monopoly of the Chinese Communist Party (CCP) was rarely in doubt, and, in particular, the PLA managed to safeguard its then limited nuclear weapons capabilities.

In the case of Pakistan and North Korea, however, political and economic dynamics differ significantly from the Chinese case or other post–Cold War nuclear concerns such as controlling fissile materials currently held by the Russian Federation. While the origins, capabilities, and overall military components of the Pakistani and North Korean nuclear weapons programs are quite different, regime transformations in Islamabad and Pyongyang, state collapse, command-and-control mechanisms in the event of regime failure, and prolonged civil-military conflicts would have fundamental implications for nuclear safeguards in both countries and, by extension, in their regions.[26]

In North Korea's case, the Kim Jong-Il regime could be overthrown by a military junta or a joint ruling body comprising key party and military leaders. In such an instance, the integrity of the command-and-control system would presumably be retained. However, in the event of prolonged intrafactional struggle within the Korean People's Army (KPA) coupled with growing civil unrest and de facto disintegration of omniscient security controls, key elements of the command structure could be unraveled. Again, while such scenarios are highly contingent on a series of developments—inability of the national command authority to function in any normal sense and which specific

---

(Continued from note 25 on preceding page) military power heralds the beginning of a second nuclear age as different from the first, that of the Cold War, as that contest was from World War II. The world that the West created is being challenged—not just in military ways but in cultural and philosophical terms as well. Just as Asia began asserting itself economically in the 1960s and 1970s, it now does so militarily, backed by arms that would make Western interference in Asia far more treacherous and costly—even in peacetime than ever before."

26 Key analysts argue that unless the Pakistani army somehow fragments beyond repair and is replaced by a rogue regime, "the likelihood of the unauthorized possession of Pakistan's nuclear weapons infrastructure is extremely small." See Sumit Ganguly, "Beyond the Nuclear Dimension: Forging Stability in South Asia," *Arms Control Today* (December 2001), www.armscontrol.org/act/2001_12/ganulynov01.asp.

forces or groups ultimately would assume control of North Korea's vast military complex, including nuclear weapons and ballistic missiles—they are a critical concern to the ROK and the United States, not to mention other regional powers. The main point here is that although the regimes that are in power in Pakistan and North Korea may not face any imminent danger of being replaced, both states exhibit many of the characteristics of failing, if not failed, states. Significant challenges to regime security would therefore have key repercussions for these two countries' WMD arsenals.

Measuring the level and depth of fatigue in states or structural corrosion is more art than science, but it is possible to identify indicators that could ultimately lead to state failure. The key, of course, is understanding the breaking point, whereby cascading series of fatigue striation would result in regime breakdown and collapse. Defining failed states, by one account, takes into consideration that the central state apparatus:

- Is not able to sustain an "effective monopoly of violence" over its territory;

- Lacks a functioning and effective judicial system in safeguarding laws and promulgating judgments that are deemed as legitimate by the international community;

- Is either unable or unwilling to comply with and fulfill international obligations; and

- Is unable or chooses not to prevent various forms of transnational economic crime or uses its territory "for the perpetration of violence against other states in the international system."[27]

In addition, a new study undertaken by *Foreign Policy* and the Fund for Peace in 2005 defined failed states as follows:

> A state is failing when its government is losing physical control of its territory or lacks a monopoly on the legitimate use of force. Other symptoms of state failure include the erosion of authority to make collective decisions, an inability to provide reasonable public services, and the loss of the

---

27 "Failed and Collapsed States in the International System," African Studies Centre, Leiden; Transnational Institute, Amsterdam; Center of Social Studies, Coimbra University; and Peace Research Center-CIP-FUHEM, Madrid, December 2003, 4.

capacity to interact in formal relations with other states as a full member of the international community. As suggested by the list of 12 indicators, extensive corruption and criminal behavior, inability to collect taxes or otherwise draw on citizen support, large-scale involuntary dislocation of the population, sharp economic decline, group-based inequality, and institutionalized persecution or discrimination are other hallmarks of state failure. States can fail at varying rates of decline through explosion, implosion or erosion.[28]

By this definition, arguments could be made that both North Korea and Pakistan may be failing rather than failed states, given that the two regimes (particularly North Korea's) do not seem to be in any imminent danger of collapse. For example, the Korean Workers' Party (KWP), under the leadership of Kim Jong-Il (and his father, the late Kim Il-Sung, before him), has been in power since 1948, and contestations to Kim's one-man Stalinist rule have so far been unable to dent the regime in any serious manner. Resilience through state terror, a nationwide security blanket, and decades of political indoctrination among other factors have led to North Korea's precarious survival. Additionally, vital Chinese aid in the form of grant assistance, oil, and food shipments have kept the regime afloat in addition to South Korean assistance to the North since the late 1990s. Thus, survivability of the North Korean regime minus external assistance from China and South Korea would be imperiled significantly. To date, there is no indication that China is contemplating any abrupt or even controlled dilution of economic or political support for North Korea or, for that matter, South Korea.

That said, North Korea, writ large, exhibits many key features of a failed state: de facto economic collapse, criminalization of the state, uneven development, pockets of famine, endemic corruption, forced migrations, and refugees. Estimates vary, given the dearth of accurate statistics, but there are at least tens of thousands of North Korean refugees in northeastern China. In the mid- to late 1990s, more than a million North Koreans are believed to have died from famine and related diseases. Internal control remains draconian and Kim Jong-Il contin-

---

28 *Foreign Policy* and Fund for Peace, "The Failed States Index," *Foreign Policy*, (July/August 2005), www.foreignpolicy.com/story/cms.php?story_id=3098.

Table 4.1. Indicators of Instability in Pakistan and North Korea

Indicators of instability	Pakistan	North Korea
Demographic pressures	5.0	8.0
Refugees and displaced persons	5.0	6.0
Group grievance	6.9	7.2
Human flight	8.0	8.1
Uneven development	9.0	9.0
Economic decline	3.3	9.6
Delegitimization of state	9.8	9.8
Public services	7.5	9.7
Human rights	8.1	9.0
Security apparatus	9.0	8.3
Fractionalized elites	9.3	8.0
External intervention	8.5	3.0

Source: Foreign Policy and the Fund for Peace, "The Failed States Index," *Foreign Policy* (July/August 2005).

ues to receive key support from the armed forces, but corruption is believed to be spreading in the KPA. Of the top 60 states listed in the 2005 "Failed States Index," 13 countries in the top 20 grouping were Asian (including Uzbekistan, Tajikistan, and Azerbaijan). North Korea ranked number 13 and Pakistan ranked 34.[29] The top 20 are considered to be "alert" states, where conditions are particularly poor, followed by the "orange" states that show key strains of failure, and finally, the "yellow" grouping that is still considered to be relatively stable. A comparison of Pakistan and North Korea is provided in table 4.1.

Table 4.1 offers only a very limited window into possible shifts in the domestic political conditions in Pakistan and India and should therefore not be construed as a prediction of acute state corrosion leading ultimately to regime or state collapse. In the case of Pakistan, domestic

---

29 Ibid. The 12 indicators in the study are: (1) mounting demographic pressures, (2) massive movement of refugees and internally displaced persons, (3) legacy of vengeance-seeking group grievance, (4) chronic and sustained human flight, (5) uneven economic development along group lines, (6) sharp and/or severe economic decline, (7) criminalization or delegitimization of the state, (8) progressive deterioration of public services, (9) widespread violation of human rights, (10) security apparatus as "state within a state," (11) rise of factionalized elites, and (12) intervention of other states or external actors.

stability remains a critical factor in tabulating the overall conditions for nuclear deterrence and the chances, however minute, of nuclear escalation in the event of a major, full-scale conventional war. While the correlation between acute state failure and the phenomenon known as the stability-instability paradox remains untested, the paradox is worth revisiting in the context of Pakistan's nuclear arsenal.

The central tenet of this paradox is that a conventional conflict is unlikely to escalate into a nuclear exchange given the enormous costs of nuclear war; hence, strategic stability is maintained. At the same time, by reducing the costs of conventional conflict, strategic stability also increases the likelihood of that conflict.[30] To date, a fairly wide-ranging consensus exists in both India and Pakistan that the paradox is likely to hold. A majority of Indian policy makers and strategic analysts believes strongly that if nuclear deterrence worked in the West throughout the Cold War, there is no reason to believe that it will not work in South Asia. Key officials have asserted that after Pakistan demonstrated itself to be a declared nuclear power, "such a move has ensured greater transparency about Pakistan's capacities and intentions. It also removes the complexes, suspicions and uncertainties about each other's nuclear capacities."[31]

Many other observers of South Asia's nuclear dilemma have asserted that strategic stability is likely to hold and that ultimately nuclear deterrence between the two states amounts to a subregional variant of the Cold War doctrine of mutually assured destruction arrived at by the United States and the Soviet Union. Diametrically divergent views are also present. Some argue forcefully that, contrary to conventional wisdom, the Indo-Pakistani nuclear standoff "do[es} not reduce or eliminate factors that contributed to past conflicts . . . Far from creating stability, these basic nuclear capabilities have led to an incomplete sense of where security lies."[32] Moreover, achieving and maintaining strate-

---

30 S. Paul Kapur, "India and Pakistan's Unstable Peace: Why Nuclear South Asia Is Not Like Cold War Europe," *International Security* 30, no. 2 (Fall 2005): 127–28.

31 Statement made by J. N. Dixit in 2002 before he became national security adviser to Indian prime minister Manmohan Singh; cited in Michael Krepon, "The Stability-Instability Paradox, Misperceptions, and Escalation Control in South Asia," in *Escalation Control and the Nuclear Option in South Asia*, ed. Michael Krepon, Rodney W. Jones, and Ziad Haider (Washington, D.C.: Henry L. Stimson Center, 2004), 5.

gic stability would also require second-strike capabilities, which India and Pakistan are lacking at the present time although sustained nuclear buildup could ultimately enable both sides to have rough parity by attaining second-strike capabilities.

One recent study has estimated that with the current inventory of ballistic missiles in South Asia, the available warning time at a minimum would be around 200 seconds.[33] Further, this study asserts that the estimated total flight time ranges from 8 to 13 minutes for ranges of 600 kilometers to 2,000 kilometers (375 miles to 1,250 miles) for missiles that are flown to full ranges. If both sides launch long-range missiles with depressed trajectories, missile flight time could be as low as 5 minutes for a 600-kilometer flight.[34] It is difficult to assess with any high degree of accuracy the actual level of deterrence integrity between Pakistan and India in the event of another major conflict. One analyst has written that, contrary to the expectations of reduced violence within the context of the stability-instability paradox, "South Asian violence has resulted from a strategic environment in which nuclear escalation is a serious possibility in the event that a limited Indo-Pakistani confrontation spirals into a full-scale conventional conflict."[35]

Escalation driven by avoiding two worst-case outcomes. The North Korean and Iranian nuclear problems present two interrelated challenges that could impact severely the future sanctity and efficacy of nonproliferation regimes. While prospects for a negotiated settlement in the Iranian and North Korean cases through the so-called EU-3 process and the six-party talks have not been irrevocably closed, both Iran and North Korea (particularly the latter) are perilously close to attaining de facto nuclear weapons status. The Iranian nuclear crisis entered a new phase with Iranian president Mahmoud Ahmadinejad's recent announcement that Iran had successfully enriched uranium for peaceful purposes.[36] The core dilemma for the United States and the

---

32 Statement by Neil Joeck, Ibid., 6.

33 M. V. Ramana, R. Rajaraman, and Zia Mian, "Nuclear Warning in South Asia: Problems and Issues," *Economic and Political Weekly*, January 17, 2004, www.epw.org.in/show/Articles.php

34 Ibid.

35 Kapur, "India and Pakistan's Unstable Peace," 151.

36 Iran's president, Mahmoud Ahmadinejad, stated on April 9, 2006, that

(Continued on next page)

EU-3 is that they are confronted with two worst-case outcomes: an Iran that moves down the road of nuclear weapons and a costly war in the event that the United States opts for a preemptive strike. The same applies in the North Korean context. Most analysts believe that North Korea already possesses two or three nuclear weapons and Pyongyang's foreign ministry announced on February 10, 2005, that it was compelled by hostile U.S. policy to "take a measure to bolster its nuclear weapons arsenal in order to protect the ideology, system, freedom and democracy chosen by its people," and, furthermore, "ha[s] manufactured nukes for self-defense . . . Its nuclear weapons will remain nuclear deterrent for self-defense under any circumstances."[37]

Thus, notwithstanding the possibility that North Korea could be dissuaded ultimately to dismantle its nuclear weapons program through the six-party talks or even bilateral U.S.–North Korean negotiations, North Korea can already be construed as a de facto nuclear weapons state. As in the case of Iran but even more so, a military option to take out North Korea's nuclear facilities would almost certainly trigger military retaliation from the North toward the South, which leads to a second worst-case scenario—a major war—that all want to avoid. In both cases, then, if one considers extreme policy measures such as a preemptive or preventive military strike to fundamentally address one worst-case outcome—nuclear-armed Iran and North Korea—it would lead to a second worst-case outcome, that is, a protracted and costly war.

Clearly, a win-win solution that would enable Iran and North Korea to accept security guarantees sufficient to dismantle their nuclear weapons ambitions would be ideal. But unless and until common denominators of security and insecurity are shared by all of the principal actors, chances of a win-win outcome are extremely unlikely. In the

---

(Continued from note 36 on preceding page) "with the blessings of God Almighty and withthe help of Iran's youth, today we perfected the A to Z of technology that is used to produce nuclear fuel and we have the capability to produce it." http://www.president.ir/eng/ahmadinejad/cronicnews/1385/01/23/index-e.htm#b5

37 Korean Central News Agency (DPRK), "DPRK FM on Its Stand to Suspend Its Participation in Six-Party Talks for Indefinite Period," February 10, 2005, www.kcna.co.jp/index-e.htm. For additional details, see "Special Report on the North Korean Nuclear Weapons Statement," Center for Nonproliferation Studies Research Story, 11 February 2005, http://cns.miis.edu/pubs/week/050211.htm.

interim, policy alternatives are going to become increasingly winnowed given the two extreme outcomes that all sides want to avoid but ultimately may not be able to.

Rise of new military (particularly asymmetrical) capabilities. Beyond the challenges posed by new breakout states or the distant possibility of nuclear escalation (however unlikely) between India and Pakistan, Asia's nuclear futures are also inextricably tied to the acquisition of more advanced conventional armaments and related military capabilities. Ironically, while the probability of a major conflict has decreased sharply since the end of the Cold War, the growing accumulation of military capital by select Asian states indicates that more robust force modernizations and increasingly sophisticated power projection platforms will be pursued. This trend is hardly surprising when taking into account the fact that accelerated economic development has enabled many key regional powers to address force deficiencies through their own mini Revolution in Military Affairs efforts.

Noteworthy also is the fact that, unlike any other region in the world, Asia is home to an intensely complex security matrix: great-power competition, emerging nuclear powers, and geopolitical hot spots—Kashmir, the Korean peninsula, and the Taiwan Strait. Further, maritime boundary disputes, increased competition for seabed energy resources, and the need to protect vital sea lanes of communication have resulted in greater emphases on naval modernizations. Capabilities-based defense planning, therefore, forms a key part of the East Asian military modernization drive that entails certain elements of a classical arms race fueled by new security dilemmas. Of key concern therefore, is the pace and depth of military modernization of the so-called militarily consequential powers in the region: China, Japan, India, the two Koreas, Taiwan, Australia, and select ASEAN states such as Singapore and Indonesia.

While the decreasing probability of major wars in East Asia is a very positive development, the emergence of hybrid conflicts or amalgamated or layered conflicts could become an increasingly salient feature of the regional security map. As such, hybrid conflicts would be characterized by the compression of conventional, unconventional, and asymmetrical capabilities; information warfare; terrorism; and even counterinsurgency. Variations of hybrid conflict can be found throughout the history of warfare, but they have gained increasing currency owing to the acceleration of asymmetrical capabilities such as WMD, ballistic and cruise missiles, information warfare, and, of late, unmanned combat air vehicles. More than ever, military forces on the ground and in command centers have to demonstrate the ability to perform increasingly complex multifaceted missions under severe operational tempo requirements. Except for U.S. forces, no regional armed force is capable of undertaking extended power projection missions. That said, as the theater of operations invariably expands owing to the introduction of new generation missiles (particularly cruise missiles), combat aircraft, and submarine forces, the militarily consequential powers of the region are bound to emphasize qualitatively advanced forces.

Although historical comparisons should always be treated with caution, the key cause for concern for twenty-first century Northeast Asia lies on the margins of new strategic rivalries. Even as East Asian states cooperate on economic matters, they may view each other as strategic rivals; and while "wars between them may not be likely, but neither will it be unthinkable."[38] Although no single, overarching security threat permeates the region, very diverse security challenges mixed with outstanding historical legacies and disputes means that "military instruments are in no danger of becoming irrelevant in Asia."[39]

Thus, what one can detect in the emerging Asian conventional force structure is the increasingly high concentration of conventional forces that are adopting in their own ways new power projection capabilities with an emphasis on acquiring asymmetrical capabilities. While the circumstances are quite different from state to state, the PLA's focus on acquiring superior information warfare fighting capabilities together with a long-overdue replacement of its aging combat aircraft; the Japanese Self Defense Forces' comprehensive force modernization programs including a strategic shift vis-à-vis China; South Korea's own mid- to long-term defense modernization programs, including next-generation combat aircraft (KFX-2), early warning aircraft (EX), and Aegis-class cruisers (KDX III); and North Korea's continuing efforts to upgrade its ballistic missile forces coupled with ongoing concerns over its nuclear weapons program suggest that almost all of the major armed forces in

---

38 Richard J. Ellings and Aaron L. Friedberg, *Strategic Asia 2001–02: Power and Purpose* (Washington, D.C.: National Bureau of Asian Research, 2001), 11.

39 Ashley J. Tellis, "Military Modernization in Asia," in *Military Modernization in an Era of Uncertainty*, ed. Ashley J. Tellis and Michael Wills (Washington, D.C.: National Bureau of Asian Research, 2005), 12.

East Asia are in the process of implementing their own versions of defense transformations. As a RAND study noted: "If or when they enter
the geopolitical arena as confident 'actors,' they may find themselves
engaged in heightened political-military competition or even conflict
with their neighbors."[40]

The acquisition of more lethal, accurate, and mobile weapons systems connected by an increasingly modernized command, control, com-
munications, computers, intelligence, surveillance, and reconnaissance
(C4ISR) system means that for the first time in history, almost all of the
mature armed forces in the region now have growing power projection capabilities. Such developments have also been spurred by latent
strategic rivalries based on the specter of a rising China and India, a
more security-conscious and militarily capable Japan, the possibility
of volatile if not violent transitions on the Korean peninsula, and potential military clashes in the Taiwan Strait or in the South China Sea.
In 2002, one noted U.S. observer wrote a still-relevant comment in the
context of Asia's military technology potential:

> The information revolution spreading around the world
> brings much more diverse sources of intelligence to the
> Asian military decision-making system. Satellites, fiber-optic
> communication lines, computer networks, and cellular
> telephone technologies disgorge information that will
> transform civil-military relations in Asia. The new informa-
> tion technologies allow a quantum jump in performance for
> key parts of the military . . . *In some areas, like jet aircraft or
> mechanized ground warfare, the Asian military is extremely
> backward compared to America or Europe. However, this assess-
> ment overlooks the role of new information technologies in making
> missile strikes and other tactics highly effective.*[41]

Early twenty-first-century East Asia is militarily significant because
for many of the key regional powers the tyranny of geography has been
overcome by advanced military technologies. To what extent emerging strategic rivalries may escalate into actual conflicts remains un-

---

40 Zalmay Khalilzad et al., *The United States and Asia: Toward a New U.S.
    Strategy and Force Posture*, report no. MR-1315-AF (Santa Monica, Calif.:
    RAND, 2001), 7.

41 Paul Bracken, *Fire in the East: The Rise of Asian Military Power and the
    Second Nuclear Age* (New York: HarperCollins, 1999), 79. Italics added.

known because one cannot assume that more robust power projection capabilities will necessarily lead to strategic instability and conflict. Friction among the great powers and between the great and lesser powers is unlikely to remain dormant.

The prominence of China's strategic footprints, more robust Japanese and South Korean air and naval assets, India's subregional ambitions, potentially volatile undercurrents in Indo-Pakistani relations, and North Korea's search to strengthen its correlation of forces may well mean that preventive political-military measures, including subregional confidence-building measures, could be brought to bear with more urgency in the region. "It is . . . easy enough to imagine events—a mismanaged crisis on the Korean peninsula or a confrontation across the Taiwan Strait or over Kashmir—that could shake strategic Asia to its core and bring powerful competitive forces, now latent, to the surface."[42]

Possible nuclear materials and nuclear technology transfers to transnational terrorist groups. To date, there has been no evidence that Pakistan, North Korea, or Iran has tried to transfer nuclear and other WMD technologies, know-how, or fissile materials to active terrorist organizations such as Al Qaeda, Jamaat-e-Islami (JI), Hizballah, or other groups. Indeed, as one U.S. analyst has noted, even the so-called rogue states that have ties with terrorists face compelling challenges not to transfer nuclear weapons or other WMD because "if the terrorists were to use these weapons against the United States or its allies, the weapons could be traced back to the donor state, which would be at risk of annihilation by an U.S. retaliatory strike. Iran's leaders have too much at stake to run this risk."[43]

Iran continues to support radical groups in Syria (such as Hizballah), and the Bush administration accuses Tehran of bankrolling and extending other resources to antigovernment terrorist groups in Iraq. For its part, although North Korea earlier was actively involved in state-sponsored terrorism (most notably the assassination of South Korea's first lady in 1974, the Rangoon bombing of 1983, and the bombing of a Korean Air Lines jet in 1987) and sporadic military incursions into South Korea still continue, Pyongyang has not launched a terrorist attack against the South since the late 1980s.

---

42 Ellings and Friedberg, *Strategic Asia 2001–02*, 23.

43 Christopher Layne, "Iran: The Logic of Deterrence," *American Conservative*, April 10, 2006, 4.

Notwithstanding virtually immediate retaliatory attacks by the United States or even allied forces in the event of foolproof evidence of transfers of nuclear components or WMD to terrorist groups by Iran or North Korea, the bigger problem is indirect transfers and breakdowns in security that could lead to unintended leaks. For instance, how much fissile material remains unaccounted for in the former Soviet republics (including Russia) is up for debate, but there is a consensus that a key risk "posed by Russia is not from a deliberate nuclear attack but from the possible leakage of its nuclear weapons or material to would-be nuclear states or terrorist groups."[44] The potential for stealing nuclear warheads, fissile materials, or the remanufacturing of warheads remains a critical facet of controlling nuclear arsenals in Russia.[45]

Although dormant today, the so-called A. Q. Khan network was responsible for transferring a host of nuclear technologies and materials to North Korea, Libya, and Pakistan. From the early 1980s until 2002, Khan and his supporters within and outside of the Pakistani armed forces provided technical assistance, including centrifuges, to Iran and North Korea although details of Khan's collaborations with Iran and North Korea have not been released by the Pakistani government. Plutonium reprocessing is believed to be one area where Khan helped North Koreans. In his public confession of February 4, 2004, Khan stated:

> The recent investigation was ordered by the Government of Pakistan consequent to the disturbing disclosures and evidence by some countries to international agencies relating to alleged proliferation activities by certain Pakistanis and foreigners over the last two decades. The investigation has established that many of the reported activities did occur, and that these were inevitably initiated at my behest. In my interviews with the concerned government officials, I was confronted with the evidence and the findings. And I have voluntarily admitted that much of it is true and accurate.[46]

44 Tom Z. Collina and Jon B. Wolfsthal, "Nuclear Terrorism and Warhead Control in Russia," *Arms Control Today*, April 2002, www.armscontrol. org/act/2002_04/colwolfapril02.asp.

45 Ibid.

46 Transcript of A. Q. Khan's speech on Pakistan Television on February 4, 2004, http://www.fas.org/nuke/guide/pakistan/nuke/aqkhan020404. html. President Musharraf subsequently fully pardoned Khan and placed him under house arrest.

Nonetheless, even after Islamabad publicly acknowledged nuclear transfers to Libya and Iran in February 2004, to date both Pakistan and North Korea have steadfastly maintained that no nuclear cooperation took place between the two countries.[47] Beginning in 1992, Pakistan and North Korea collaborated extensively on ballistic missile technology transfers in return for nuclear expertise. By the mid-1990s, the North Koreans provided a virtual wholesale transfer of its No-dong missile, which was subsequently readapted as Pakistan's Ghauri missile.[48] It is believed that Khan began to transfer nuclear technologies to North Korea in 1997 or 1998 through 2003. During his public confession in 2004, Khan admitted to at least 13 visits to North Korea.[49]

Although not independently verified, intelligence officials in the United States and Europe (Germany, for example) believe that Khan "may have supplied North Korea with old and discarded centrifuge and enrichment machines together with sets of drawings, sketches, technical data, and depleted uranium hexafluoride."[50] The sheer scale and magnitude of the A. Q. Khan network brings to the fore two critical issues: the extent of secondary proliferation, and the possible transfer of technologies and materials to terrorist groups or to intermediaries that could ultimately provide critical know-how to terrorist groups such as Al Qaeda and its allies.

Existing nonproliferation regimes and watchdogs such as the IAEA were inadequate in detecting the global reach of the Khan network, although there were indications throughout the 1980s and 1990s that the network was selling expertise and equipment to three key states: Iran, North Korea, and Libya. Ironically, the extent of the Khan network was not exposed until Libya's surprising about-face on its WMD

---

47 Richard P. Cronin, K. Alan Kronstadt, and Sharon Squassoni, *Pakistan's Nuclear Proliferation Activities and the Recommendations of the 9/11 Commission: U.S. Policy Constraints and Options* (Washington, D.C.: Congressional Research Service, January 25, 2005), 14; see also John Lancaster, "Pakistan Says 3 Nuclear Scientists Are under Investigation; 'Greed' May Have Been Motivating Factor, Spokesman Says," *Washington Post* Foreign Service, December 23, 2003, www.washingtonpost.com/wp-dyn/articles/A24087-2003Dec23.html.

48 Michael Laufer, "A. Q. Khan Nuclear Chronology," *Proliferation Brief* 8, no. 8 (September 7, 2005), 5.

49 Ibid., 6.

50 Ibid.

programs: the Khan Research Laboratory became a one-stop shopping center for blueprints and full centrifuge assemblies, low-enriched uranium, and even (to Libya) nuclear weapons design,[51] and there is no guarantee that any of these materials or know-how ultimately did not reach Al Qaeda, the Taliban, or sympathizing groups and organizations. Although unproved, suspicions linger that elements of the Khan network "may have helped al Qaeda obtain nuclear secrets prior to the fall of the Taliban regime in Afghanistan."[52]

Asian WMD Profiles: China, India, Pakistan, and North Korea

It comes as no surprise that Asia's WMD future depends critically on how the four major members of the nuclear club—three declared and one virtual breakout state—interact not only among themselves but in their individual and at times collective interactions with the United States, Japan, and the two Koreas. The linkage between nuclear weapons and regime survival—linked with, although not necessarily the same as, state survival—is most pronounced in the case of North Korea, which further complicates the WMD map of Asia. Admittedly, Pakistan's and India's nuclear weapons also play crucial roles in bolstering regime prestige, providing coercive political leverage in select circumstances, and offering regime security in the broader sense of a security umbrella however vulnerable they may be to key undercurrents alluded to before. Yet, in the case of North Korea, there is no discernable differentiation or distinction between state and regime survival. For Kim Jong-Il, his immediate family, and a handful of the top leadership, the ability of the regime to survive and prosper is synonymous with state survival. Should the regime falter or—in the worst-case scenario for Kim Jong-Il—collapse, maintaining command and control integrity in addition to securing all nuclear and WMD facilities and arsenals is going to arise as the most important issue on the Ko-

---

51 For a detailed account of Khan's role, see Sharon Squassoni, "Closing Pandora's Box: Pakistan's Role in Nuclear Proliferation," *Arms Control Today*, April 2004, www.armscontrol.org/act/2004_04/Squassoni.asp.

52 David Albright, "Unraveling the A. Q. Khan and Future Proliferation Networks," *Washington Quarterly* 28, no. 2 (Spring 2005): 112.

rean peninsula together with avoiding accidental war or prolonged civil conflict and turmoil in the North.

Understanding the WMD profile map of the region thus represents a maze in more ways. One must understand three major interlocking challenges:

- **There is a lack of credible intelligence, particularly in the context of North Korea's WMD and nuclear weapons programs.** All of the known and publicly available intelligence on North Korea's nuclear capability is based on a combination of best estimates and technical sources and, even here, one can readily detect differences among the United States, South Korean, Chinese, and Japanese assessments. Overall intelligence vis-à-vis Iran's burgeoning nuclear program or, for that matter, India's and Pakistan's nuclear assets is highly unlikely to be considerably better than intelligence about North Korea although the world today knows significantly more about the Indo-Pakistani arsenals following their tests in 1998.

- **The range of WMD arsenals under consideration, including nuclear, chemical, and biological weapons in addition to ballistic missiles, means that even if one successfully isolates the nuclear problem, it is intrinsically difficult because it has to be calibrated with other WMD assets.** This is particularly true of North Korea. As the on-and-off U.S.–North Korean missile talks have shown, the basket approach to negotiations—that is, moving from one area to the next if discord persists in one "basket"—reminiscent of Commission on Security and Cooperation in Europe negotiations in the 1970s and 1980s cannot really be duplicated.

- **The principal actors, particularly allies, have contrasting political perceptions.** As a case in point, ROK-U.S. relations have ebbed and flowed since the late 1990s, and this has been especially true since the beginning of the Roh Moo-Hyun government in March 2003. Although the most excessive expressions of anti-Americanism are no longer as pervasive as in 2002–03, the critical point is the gap within South Korea and between South Korea and the United States on North Korea. Gen. Leon J. LaPorte, commander of the U.S. Forces Korea, testified to the Congress in March 2003:

> Many South Koreans under age 45, a generation that has lived in an era of peace and prosperity, have little or no understanding of the North Korean threat. These South

Koreans perceive North Korea not as a threat but rather as a Korean neighbor, potential trading partner and a country that provides access to expanded Eurasian markets. *This perception of North Korea contrasts with America's view that North Korea is a threat to regional and global stability. This divergent view of North Korea, coupled with strong national pride, has been a cause of periodic tension in the Republic of Korea–United States alliance* . . . Demonstrations against U.S. policy and military presence increased sharply during this year's Republic of Korea presidential election. Political interest groups made claims of inequity in the Republic of Korea-United States alliance a central issue in the presidential campaign.[53]

These challenges differ from subregion to subregion and from alliance to alliance, but they cannot be ignored in assessing future paths of Asian WMD. Potent political forces and divides could become increasingly visible in handling Asian WMD issues, especially if the situation deteriorates markedly in North Korea or Pakistan. With these points in mind, a brief profile of the major players in the WMD game is provided below with an emphasis on the North Korean nuclear program and related WMD programs.

PRC's Nuclear Capabilities and Proliferation Activities

China's PLA is well into its third decade of a comprehensive and targeted military modernization and transformation program that began in earnest after the Sino-Vietnamese border clash of 1979.[54] The PLA's modernization efforts since the early 1990s can be best described as stealth transformation in that even as the top political and military leadership stress the need for China's military to catch up with other great

---

53 "Statement of Leon J. LaPorte, Commander United Nations Command, Commander, Republic of Korea-United States Combined Forces Command and United States Forces Korea, Before the 108th Congress, Senate Armed Services Committee, Washington, D.C., March 13, 2003, 3-4," http://armed-services.senate.gov/statemnt/2003/March/LaPorte.pdf. Italics added.

54 Lt. Col. Dennis J. Blasko, "Chinese Army Modernization: An Overview," *Military Review* (September-October 2005), http://usacac.leavenworth.army.mil/cac/milreview/download/English/SEPOCT05/blasko.pdf.

powers (principally though by no means limited to the United States), neither does it want to become a magnet or target for regional force buildups that could severely narrow or even marginalize its postreform military gains. Overcoming key deficiencies in China's force structure and its ability to wage a range of combined military operations means that, for the time being, China can ill afford to antagonize constituent states in its vicinity or other regional great powers such as Japan and India.

Thus, the PLA has emphasized asymmetric programs by leveraging its advantages while exploiting the vulnerabilities of possible adversaries.[55] In turn, as the PLA continues to modernize, two key misperceptions may lead to miscalculations or crises: underestimating the degree to which Chinese forces have been modernized, and overestimating their own forces' operational capability and adaptability.[56] Compared with the United States, China's military footprint continues to be focused in its immediate environs because it does not have foreign military bases or the logistical capacity to maintain long-term and long-range offshore military operations. Chinese defense elites are concerned about protecting its core sovereign zones (including the South China Sea and Taiwan) in addition to strategic pivots such as the Sino–North Korean border that could severely undermine China's security.[57]

According to estimates made by the U.S. Department of Defense in addition to open-source estimates such as those made by the Carnegie Endowment for International Peace and the Center for Nonproliferation Studies, China as of 2005 had a total of approximately 410 nuclear warheads that are believed to be divided into some 250 "strategic" weapons maintained in a triad of land-based missiles, bombers, and SLBMs (table 4.2). In addition, China is believed to possess some 150 tactical nuclear weapons.[58] China's strategic nuclear forces are deployed in some 20 locations under the command of the Central Military Commission (CMC). For its part, the U.S. Department of Defense recently

---

55 *Annual Report to Congress, The Military Power of the People's Republic of China 2005* (Washington, D.C.: U.S. Department of Defense, 2005), 26.

56 Ibid.

57 Blasko, "Chinese Army Modernization: An Overview," 69.

58 "China Profile: Nuclear Capabilities," Nuclear Threat Initiative, Washington, D.C., December 2005, www.nuclearthreatinitiative.com/ e_research/profiles/China/Nuclear/5569_5636.html.

Table 4.2. Nuclear Weapons Countries, 2005

Country	Total nuclear warheads
NPT nuclear weapons states	
China	410
France	350
Russia	~16,000
United Kingdom	200
United States	~10,300
Non-NPT nuclear weapons states	
India	75–110[a]
Israel	100–170[b]
Pakistan	50–110[c]
Suspected nuclear weapons states	
North Korea	n.a.
Suspected clandestine program	
Iran	n.a.

Source: Carnegie Endowment for International Peace, http://www.carnegieendowment.org/images/npp/nuke.jpg.

a For India, the number or actual weapons assembled or capable of being assembled is unknown although India is thought to have produced enough weapons-grade plutonium to produce between 75 and 110 nuclear weapons.

b For Israel, the number or actual weapons assembled or capable of being assembled is unknown but is likely to be at the lower end of the range stated.

c For Pakistan, the number or actual weapons assembled or capable of being assembled is unknown although India may have produced enough weapons-grade uranium to produce up to 110 nuclear weapons.

---

noted that China is "fielding more survivable missiles capable of targeting India, Russia, virtually all of the United States, and the Asian-Pacific theater as far south as Australia and New Zealand."[59]

It is estimated that the PRC has 20 or so ICBMs (CSS-4 ICBMs); 100 are thought to be deployed on missiles and bombers. China's other strategic assets include the mobile DF-31 and the DF-31A ICBMs (initial operational capacity [IOC] by September 2007) and the sea-based JL-2 SLBMs (IOC October 2008).[60] The PRC also has the CSS-5 medium-

---

59 *Annual Report to Congress, The Military Power of the People's Republic of China 2005,* 28.

60 Ibid.

range ballistic missiles for regional contingencies. To date, China has not disclosed that it has tactical nuclear weapons—that is, low-yield bombs, artillery shells, short-range missiles, and atomic demolition munitions—but the PLA is believed to be emphasizing key precision strike capabilities, including short-range ballistic missiles, land-attack cruise missiles, air-to-surface missiles, and antiship cruise missiles.

While the mission of constraining U.S. operations in the Asia-Pacific region looms as a significant priority for the PRC's strategic forces, China's nuclear weapons also provide a critical dividend for its broader Asian strategy. Although Sino-Indian relations have improved over the past several years, China sees improved U.S.-Indian ties and the July 2005 U.S.-India nuclear agreement as counterbalancing whatever advantages its strategic forces would have against an Indian contingency or, at the very least, containing more aggressive Indian forays in the Indian Ocean and the Bay of Bengal. In October 2005, China strongly criticized the United States for making an exception for India—accepting India as the sixth declared nuclear weapon state—in exchange for India's selective opening up of civilian nuclear facilities to international and U.S. inspection.[61]

Unsurprisingly, Indian strategists share a relatively broad consensus with mainstream U.S. perceptions on China's core strategic objectives vis-à-vis East Asia. To be sure, divergences of views are very evident in India on China's strategic ambitions, but many have voiced strikingly similar views on the broad contours of Chinese strategy aired in the West.

One recent analysis pinned down China's grand strategy in Asia on four main pillars: (1) regaining sovereignty over Taiwan, (2) expanding its military presence in the South China Sea, (3) inducing the withdrawal of forward-positioned U.S. forces from East Asia, and (4) keeping Japan in a state of perpetual strategic subordination.[62] Furthermore,

---

61 More recently, however, the U.S.-India deal has faced key hurdles from the U.S. Congress, and the Bush administration has insisted that India cannot pursue the same nuclear policy as the five declared nuclear powers. For more details, see Brahma Chellaney, "Vaunted U.S.-India Nuclear Deal Begins to Fall Apart," *International Herald Tribune*, February 13, 2006.

62 Subhash Kapila, "China's Grand Strategy and Military Modernisation," South Asia Analysis Group, paper no. 642, March 26, 2003, www.saag.org/papers7/paper647.html.

it was noted that "after East Asia, China has focused her undivided attention on south Asia. India's natural pre-eminence and strategic power potential is an anathema to China. In China's perceptions, India alone can challenge China's 'Grand Strategy' of emerging as the sole dominant power in Asia."[63] India's nuclear explosion in 1974 was therefore premised on two fronts: the need to respond to China's own nuclear arsenals ever since it became a nuclear weapons state in 1964 and to forestall sustained Chinese support for Pakistan as the regional "spoiler state" in challenging Indian supremacy in South Asia.

Although it goes without saying that India's own strategic ambitions compelled Pakistan to commit itself to a crash nuclear weapons program, it is also important to keep in mind that China played a key role in relaying crucial technology and know-how to Pakistan in addition to North Korea and Iran. In November 2000, China announced its commitment to adhering to similar guidelines contained in the Missile Technology Control Regime (MTCR) provisions insofar as missile sales to third countries are concerned, and it published those regulations and guidelines in August 2002.[64] Of key concern is China's suspected transfer of nuclear and missile technologies to Pakistan, North Korea, and Iran. U.S. intelligence confirmed in September 1999, for example, that Pakistan obtained the M-11 short-range ballistic missile from China and that a number of Chinese firms were suspected.[65] China's collaboration with North Korea on both nuclear technologies and missile technologies has often aired key concerns of secondary proliferation.

India's and Pakistan's Nuclear Arsenals

One of the key discernable differences in the nuclear strategies of China, India, and Pakistan is the gradual shift from a global focus to a regional focus to a subregional focus. Even as China continues to espouse a non-first-use nuclear doctrine and its overall arsenal is significantly smaller than those of the United States and Russia, there is little doubt that China's nuclear posture takes into account both strategic and tactical capabilities and targets. For India, nuclear weapons provide a strategic equalizer against what it perceives as Chinese moves to constrain In-

---

63 Ibid.

64 Shirley A. Kan, "China and Proliferation of Weapons of Mass Destruction and Missiles: Policy Issues" (Washington, D.C.: Congressional Research Service, April 4, 2005), 2.

65 Ibid., 10.

dian maneuverability in its own backyard while they also check Pakistan's military pressures. Since it began its nuclear weapons program in 1968, just four years after China's successful test, and particularly since it conducted its so-called peaceful nuclear explosion in 1974 (a label that was possible owing to a loophole in its earlier nuclear cooperation agreement with Canada), India has maintained the unfairness of the Nuclear Non-Proliferation Treaty (NPT) system and has refused to be a signatory.

Since India has never released data on its nuclear forces, it is impossible to say with any degree of certainty how many warheads India deems necessary to maintain its minimum-credible-deterrent posture or when it hopes to achieve the requisite force level to achieve this objective. According to an estimate made by the *Bulletin of Atomic Scientists,* India is believed to have a stockpile of 40–50 assembled warheads although *Defense News* reported in late 2004 that according to an Indian defense official, India will likely have 300–400 nuclear and thermonuclear weapons based on a fully operational triad system.[66]

The fact that India's nuclear forces are targeted primarily against China and Pakistan whereas Pakistan's are exclusively India-specific means that New Delhi's weapons program is significantly larger than Pakistan's and continues to seek more advanced platforms.[67] Boosted fission and thermonuclear warheads, long-range ballistic and cruise missiles, and, in the long run, sea-based capabilities (submarine-launched ballistic or cruise missiles) are some of the areas India is currently working on.[68] Since the tests in 1998, the two sides have begun to transform their forces into operational nuclear forces, including aircraft-delivered nuclear bombs and short- and intermediate-range ballistic missiles. Some analysts have noted that, compared with India, Pakistan may be ahead in developing a nuclear command and control system that takes into account operational use of nuclear weapons, but this cannot be verified.[69]

---

66 Cited in Robert S. Norris and Hans M. Kristensen, "India's Nuclear Forces, 2005," *Bulletin of Atomic Scientists* 61, no. 5 (September/October 2005): 73.

67 Gaurav Kampani, "Seven Years after the Nuclear Tests: Appraising South Asia's Nuclear Realities," *NTI Issue Brief,* June 2005, www.nti.org/e_research/e3_64a.html.

68 Ibid.

69 Ibid.

In the context of South Asia's strategic environment, three key points should be noted in India's "cold start" war doctrine, introduced on April 28, 2004:

- An apparent shift from defensive to offensive operations mode so that India now is poised to undertake offensive actions against Pakistan, a proxy actor in the region, or terrorists against India;

- An intent to conduct offensive operations at the early stages of conflict to prevent Pakistan from counting on foreign intervention and or support;

- An implicit strategy that could take into consideration military intervention or even preemptive strikes.[70]

India currently is nearing full-fledged nuclear power status based on its emerging nuclear triad. India's Ministry of Defense, in its annual report in 2005, noted that India's nuclear doctrine is "based on the principle of minimum credible deterrence and no-first-use as opposed to doctrines or postures of launch on warning."[71]

Notwithstanding such shifts in Indian military logic, it does not necessarily follow that India will undertake preemptive military strikes or that relations with Pakistan or, for that matter, with China will inevitably deteriorate. For instance, in the aftermath of the December 13, 2001, terrorist attacks on the Indian parliament and ensuing tensions between Pakistan and India on the issue of cross-border terrorism, both sides engaged in nuclear signaling but, in the midst of tensions, New Delhi and Islamabad exchanged navigational coordinates of their nuclear installations based on the December 1988 Agreement on the Prohibition of Attack against Nuclear Installations and Facilities.[72]

For Pakistan, key military concerns are lack of strategic depth in the context of its inferior conventional forces and the need to offset India's robust ambitions in South Asia as the most powerful state. Like

---

70 Subhash Kapila, "Indian Army Validates Its Cold Start War Doctrine," South Asia Analysis Group, paper no. 1408, June 7, 2005, www.saag.org/papers15/paper 1408.html.

71 Robert S. Norris and Hans M. Kristensen, "India's Nuclear Forces, 2005," 73.

72 Rahul Roy-Chaudhury, "Nuclear Doctrine, Declaratory Policy, and Escalation Control," in *Escalation Control and the Nuclear Option in South Asia*, ed. Michael Krepon, Rodney W. Jones, and Ziad Haider (Washington, D.C.: Henry L. Stimson Center, 2004), 105.

India, Pakistan is not a signatory to the NPT and insists that its nuclear program is designed for deterrence against India. Pakistan's nuclear program began soon after India's 1974 test and embarked on a highly enriched uranium (HEU) bomb. By 1989–90 the United States concluded that Pakistan was on the verge of assembling a first-generation nuclear device.[73] Again, like India, Pakistan does not release any nuclear weapons data, but outside experts estimate that Pakistan has between 24 and 48 nuclear weapons and has produced enough fissile material to produce 30–52 nuclear weapons.[74] Insofar as delivery vehicles are concerned, Pakistan has reverse engineered both Chinese and North Korean missiles such as the No-dong missile with its 1,500-kilometer (930-mile) range, which is called the Ghauri in Pakistan. Pakistan also acquired the short-range (300 kilometers, or 185 miles) M-11 missile from China. By the late 1990s, it is believed that China provided assistance to Pakistan to help develop the solid-fueled Shaheen-1 missile (with a range of 750 kilometers or 465 miles) which was last tested in October 2002.[75]

For the time being, the Indo-Pakistani rivalry is in a gray zone exhibiting realization that any move toward nuclear escalation would result in catastrophic consequences, but neither side is yet prepared to undertake a fundamental reappraisal of its nuclear policies and strategies. On the more positive side, India and Pakistan understand the inherent dangers of shifting to launch-on-warning modes, which both sides have studiously avoided. To the extent that pragmatic technocrats on both sides are in charge of the broader command-and-control system, abrupt changes in nuclear policies are unlikely.

More fundamentally, however, a margin for error exists in terms of breaks in safeguards against accident or interference and preventing leakage as well as secondary proliferation.[76] Both sides retain governmental control (more specifically the military in Pakistan's case) over

---

73 "Pakistan Profile," Nuclear Threat Initiative, Washington, D.C., February 2006, http://www.nuclearthreatinitiative.com/e_research/profiles/Pakistan/index.html.

74 Robert S. Norris, Hans M. Kristensen, and Joushua Handler, "Pakistan's Nuclear Forces, 2001," *Bulletin of Atomic Scientists* 58, no. 1 (January/February 2001), 70.

75 Ibid.

76 Michael Quinlan, "India-Pakistan Deterrence Revisited," *Survival* 47, no. 3 (Autumn 2005): 111.

their nuclear arsenals, but, as India moves to a full-fledged nuclear capability, Pakistan's vulnerabilities could increase, perhaps significantly. In the case of Pakistan, the most egregious mistake it made was that the A. Q. Khan network would not have succeeded without implicit support from the highest echelons of the armed forces, who were most likely imbued with pride over becoming the first Muslim state with nuclear powers. One hopes that the secularization of Pakistan's nuclear weapons programs continues, although this is not assured.

North Korea's Quest for Nuclear Weapons

A decade after the outbreak of the first North Korean nuclear crisis in 1993, the Korean peninsula and the world are once again grappling with the North Korean nuclear quagmire and, by extension, the broader "Korean question." To outside observers, Pyongyang's renewed brinkmanship makes little, if any sense. Kim Jong-Il's experiment with limited market reforms and his initial forays in normalization talks with Japan and North Korea's establishment of full diplomatic ties with EU member states (and the renormalization of relations with Australia) seemed to suggest that North Korea was moving cautiously to a mini-version of post-Mao reforms in China.

Pyongyang's announcement of the Sinuiju special economic zone and the promise to develop Kaesong city and the Kumgang mountain resort among other projects were perceived by South Korea's Kim Dae-Jung government (1998–2003) and the Roh Moo-Hyun administration as positive indicators of North Korean reforms and, equally significant, vindication of their protracted policy of comprehensive engagement with the North. Nevertheless, the commencement of the second North Korean nuclear crisis differs qualitatively from the original crisis that began in early 1993 when North Korea announced that it would withdraw from the NPT.[77]

---

77 Since North Korea announced its withdrawal from the NPT on January 10, 2003, soon after the IAEA passed a resolution on January 6 calling upon the DPRK to abide fully by previous IAEA resolutions regarding nuclear safeguard protocols, North Korea has no longer been a member of the NPT. In defending its decision, Pyongyang declared an "automatic and immediate effectuation of its withdrawal from the NPT," nullifying its earlier moratorium of June 1993. See "Text of North Korea's Statement on NPT Withdrawal," KCNA New Agency, Pyongyang, January 10, 2003, http://cns.miis.edu/research/korea/npstate.htm.

Despite North Korea's announcement on February 10, 2005, that it had chosen to "increase its nuclear arsenal" owing to a series of hostile moves on the part of the United States and that it was postponing indefinitely its participation in the six-party talks, North Korea returned to the talks during the fourth round in August and September 2005. Subsequently, in a joint statement, "the DPRK (Democratic Peoples Republic of Korea) committed to abandoning all nuclear weapons and existing nuclear programs and returning, at an early date, to the Treaty on the Non-Proliferation of Nuclear Weapons and to IAEA safeguards" and, for its part, "the United States affirmed that it has no nuclear weapons on the Korean peninsula and has no intention to attack or invade the DPRK with nuclear or conventional weapons."[78]

The joint statement also noted that "the ROK reaffirmed its commitment not to receive or deploy nuclear weapons in accordance with the 1992 Joint Declaration of the Denuclearization of the Korean Peninsula, while reaffirming that there exist no nuclear weapons within its territory."[79] As of April 2006, discussions are continuing in Beijing and elsewhere between the United States and North Korea to restart the six-party talks, but Pyongyang has not provided any public assurance that it will rejoin the talks. How long this impasse is going to last is difficult to assess because North Korea is known for last-minute brinkmanship, and intelligence on North Korea's nuclear program should be received with caution. Some of the more basic contours of the North Korean nuclear problem are now presented.

Although North Korea has not demonstrated its nuclear weapons capability through an underground test, it probably possesses two to four nuclear weapons and is capable of producing significantly larger numbers of nuclear weapons. For all intents and purposes, North Korea is a de facto nuclear weapons state although it is clearly not in Pakistan's league. According to a U.S. National Intelligence Council report issued in December 2001,[80] "the U.S. intelligence

---

78 "Joint Statement on the Fourth Round of the Six-Party Talks,"
    September 19, 2005, http://usinfo.state.gov/eap/Archive/2005/Sep/19-
    210095.html.

79 Ibid.

80 "North Korea Profile," Nuclear Threat Initiative, Washington, D.C.,
    December 2005, www.nuclearthreatinitiative.com/e_research/profiles/
    NK/index.html.

community ascertained in the mid-1990s that North Korea had produced one, possibly two, nuclear weapons." In October 2002, North
Korea confirmed (and subsequently backtracked on the confirmation)
earlier U.S. intelligence assessments that North Korea was working on
a clandestine HEU program. If these assessments are correct, ongoing
efforts to dissuade North Korea from pursuing nuclear weapons have,
in a significant way, already failed. This is not to suggest that the six-
party talks should be scrapped; only that the often-stated policy objective of "zero tolerance" vis-à-vis North Korea's nuclear weapons has
been weakened substantially in certain respects by intelligence assessments made by the United States in addition to North Korea's own
announcements that it is nuclear weapons capable.

On the basis of the 5 MWe reactor at Yongbyon, many observers
believe North Korea extracted approximately 8.4 kilograms (18.5
pounds) of weapons-grade plutonium before 1994 (one to two nuclear
weapons' worth), approximately 25 kilograms (55 pounds) in 2003 (four
to six nuclear weapons' worth), and 10–14 kilograms (22–31 pounds)
in 2005 (two nuclear weapons' worth). As of November 2005, North
Korea is estimated to have 43 ± 10 kilograms (95 pounds ± 22 pounds)
of separated plutonium. From 2005 onwards, it could have 5-7 kilograms (11–22 pounds) per year (1+ weapon per yr). In the future, North
Korea could produce up to 60 kilograms (132 pounds) per year (for
approximately 10 weapons annually).[81]

**It is unlikely that security assurances provided by the United
States or in unison with South Korea can ultimately guarantee the
survivability of the North Korean regime.** Many have argued that
North Korea's fundamental quest for nuclear weapons stems from its
deeply rooted sense of insecurity, ranging from shifting security guarantees from its major patrons (the Soviet Union and China) during the
Cold War, to the sustained U.S. military presence in South Korea, and
to the unique features of the North Korean communist state.[82] The
United States has stated on numerous occasions that it has neither the
intention nor the desire to wage war with North Korea. Some strate-

---

81 Siegfried S. Hecker, "Technical Summary of DPRK Nuclear Program,"
    Carnegie Endowment for International Peace (presented at the Non-
    Proliferation Conference, Washington, D.C., November 8, 2005).

82 Murray Hiebert, "Pyongyang Long Sought Atomic Bomb," *Wall Street
    Journal*, May 18, 2005, Sec. A.

gists and policy makers (primarily in South Korea) have urged the United States to sign a nonaggression accord or agreement with North Korea as the first step toward the creation of a peace regime on the Korean peninsula. The survival of the Kim dynasty, however, will in the end depend on the Kim regime's ability to perpetuate the dynasty through its domestic policies rather than through external security guarantees.

North Korea is both an instigator and a beneficiary of secondary proliferation, which has already set into place a series of strategic consequences. North Korea already has in place the most advanced and aggressive ballistic missile program and has transferred core technologies, if not wholesale missiles, to numerous states such as Egypt, Syria, Iraq, Iran, Libya, and Yemen. Pakistan's and Iran's ballistic missiles have benefited significantly from North Korea's technological support, which, in turn, has provided these states with important force multipliers in their respective WMD programs. The A. Q. Khan network demonstrated the extent to which existing nonproliferation regimes were woefully inadequate in forestalling, much less preventing, severe proliferation leakages. North Korea may also be receiving important flight test data from missiles tested in other countries such as Iran and Pakistan.[83] And, although there is no verifiable intelligence, Pakistan also may have shared its May 1998 underground nuclear test information with North Korea. Insofar as its missile arsenal is concerned, Pyongyang is unlikely to negotiate it away for the following reasons:

- Ballistic missiles serve as key force multipliers for the Korean People's Army (KPA) in order to offset any South Korean advances in the conventional sector.

- Ballistic missiles serve a key function as strategic buffers against the South, the United States, and Japan because Scud-B/C missiles can reach almost all South Korean targets, and the No-dong-1 missile, with a range of 1,350 kilometers (840 miles), can reach parts of Japan. The Taepo-dong-1 missile, with a range of 4,000 kilometers (2,500 miles), can theoretically reach parts of western Alaska. If

---

83 Joseph Cirincione, Jon B. Wolfsthal, and Miriam Rajkumar, *Deadly Arsenals: Nuclear, Biological and Chemical Threats*, rev. ed. (Washington, D.C.: Carnegie Endowment for International Peace, 2005), 241.

North Korea successfully develops the Taepodong-2, with a range of up to 6,000 kilometers (3,725 miles), it will have intercontinental capabilities. Combined, these missiles provide the North with strategic capabilities against not only South Korea but also Japan and even the United States.

- North Korea's ballistic missiles, like its nuclear weapons program, are tied inextricably with regime survival.

North Korea has pursued its nuclear and ballistic missile programs since the 1960s, significantly before regime survival purportedly depended on external security guarantees. Given the underlying strategic, political, and military utility of North Korea's ballistic missiles and its nuclear weapons program, chances are not high that North Korea is going to bargain away the very assets that are prolonging the regime as well as the state. Divorcing North Korea's nuclear and ballistic missile arsenals from regime survival is central to implementing a viable drawdown and verifiable dismantlement of these two core programs. That said, not unlike Pakistan but also Iran, North Korea has the desire to acquire a range of asymmetrical weapons systems that can perhaps be traced to deeply rooted conceptions of independence mixed with intrinsically North Korean political values and interests. It is crucial to appreciate the fact that the nuclear weapons program began under Kim Il-Sung, during an era when arguably North Korea received the highest level of support from both its patron states.

In the near term, how the second North Korean nuclear crisis ultimately unfolds could have a major impact on rethinking South Korea's security options. Recent political changes in South Korea indicate that, even if North Korea were to cross the nuclear weapons threshold by conducting an underground test or by discarding its self-imposed long-range ballistic missile test moratorium, Seoul is highly unlikely to join efforts such as sanctions or even very limited military action that might be seen as threatening to the North and thus reflect negatively on prospects for South-North rapprochement.

Other triggering factors could include a marked shift in South Korea's security consensus based on a rapid acceleration of inter-Korean reconciliation leading toward a de facto unified state. Insofar as the nuclear issue is concerned, five interrelated forces continue to complicate its resolution, and by extension, the broader contours of the South-North equation:

- Changing domestic politics in South Korea and an increasingly bifurcated security consensus;

- Tensions in the Korean-U.S. relationship that are unlikely to dissipate any time in the near future;

- New challenges to effective policy coordination among the United States, South Korea, and Japan;

- Pyongyang's own strategic choices pursuant to rising international pressure against North Korea's nuclear ambitions; and

- Actions that could be undertaken by the United States in consort with its key allies short of force if the six-party talks or parallel bilateral discussions ultimately prove unsuccessful.

Compared with the first North Korean nuclear crisis from March 1993 when North Korea announced its withdrawal from the NPT until October 1994 when the U.S.–North Korea Agreed Framework was signed, the second nuclear crisis continues to unfold under very different circumstances, including a sea change in South Korean attitudes toward the North in general and the nature of the North Korean military threat in particular.

All policy choices ultimately entail costs, and were South Korea to fundamentally depart from the United States over the North Korean nuclear issue, a range of side effects would emerge. First, above and beyond the currently envisioned force reductions by 2007–08, a further reduction in U.S. forces is entirely possible. In turn, the cumulative defense burden for the ROK would also inevitably increase. At the same time, the lack of strategic intelligence provided by the United States would, in all likelihood, be detrimental to South Korea's longer-term defense and security needs.

For the foreseeable future, it is highly unlikely that South Korea would be able to operationalize strategic intelligence platforms in the absence of key U.S. intelligence data. In addition, if South Korea pursues a security policy strategy that does not include the U.S. alliance as a central pillar and if Washington chooses to withdraw its forces from South Korea, Japan would likely emerge as the key front state in Northeast Asia. At the same time, the economic impact of a U.S. troop withdrawal would have to factor into South Korea's economic and political calibrations, given the potentially adverse correlation with sustained foreign direct investment in South Korea and foreign private sector lending to Korean firms. Last but not least, absent a U.S. security umbrella, South Korea would have no choice but to cope directly with a potentially more aggressive China, particularly as it goes into the so-called unification tunnel, and securing alternative security arrangements could be highly problematic for South Korea.

Concluding Remarks

Asia's entry into the twenty-first century lies in marked contrast to the ruptures that ensued a century ago in China and Korea following decades of dynastic decay and ultimately collapse. That these collapses were accelerated by Japan's post-Meiji imperialism and colonialism is not in doubt, only that domestic political forces as much as external threats to security jointly resulted in the reshaping of the East Asian strategic landscape for a half century.

Just as the end of World War II ushered in a new world with regionwide ramifications, the accumulation of unparalleled economic wealth and military capital by a growing cadre of Asian powers, the potent mix of new political and strategic undercurrents, and pronounced though not readily visible vulnerabilities could serve today to radically alter the emerging balance of interests. Fortunately, however, classical balance-of-power politics among the great powers, reminiscent of the nineteenth century's Concert of Europe, is highly unlikely to be duplicated in Asia. Structural preconditions, political will, flexibility in key institutions, and, most of all, deeply entrenched historical memories along critical geopolitical pivots diminish any serious replay of late-nineteenth-century European politics. Moreover, the preponderance of U.S. power throughout much of the region and the inability of any single Asian state to contest U.S. military supremacy mean that, for the time being, a theater peer worthy of its name is not going to appear on the horizon.

The ability of the United States together with its allies to prevent key fault lines from erupting into streams of instability or pockets of conflicts is going to be tested more thoroughly than at any other time since the web of U.S.-led alliances was forged in the aftermath of the Korean conflict. Unlike in the early 1950s, the United States today confronts a region with unprecedented levers of power and influence and political conditions that dictate new rule sets for alliance management. But it is precisely in these tipping-point zones where the beneficial elements of U.S. power can foster constructive and, by extension, more peaceful change.

The success of containment in Europe and Asia during the Cold War was premised on essentially linear, though costly, interventions as evinced by the Korean and Vietnamese conflicts. In the Asia of the early twenty-first century, a strategic consensus akin to the fight against communism is absent. This is the real litmus test for the United States, its allies, and states of consequence in the Asia-Pacific region. The forging of a new consensual strategic doctrine is therefore perhaps the first step toward revamping Asia's security architecture well into the twenty-first century.

Comment

Challenge of Deterring Nuclear Proliferation

Pierre Goldschmidt

The greater the number of states possessing nuclear weapons, the greater the risk that, one day, by design or by accident and with catastrophic consequences, the weapons will be used or will fall into the hands of nonstate actors.

We must therefore reject as irresponsible the idea that the international community should get used to the fact that sooner or later more countries will possess nuclear weapons and that we can do nothing about it. Rather, it is essential to take all the necessary steps to prevent and deter nonnuclear weapons states (NNWS) from acquiring such weapons.

Prevention entails persuading a state (both the leaders and the people) that it is not in that state's best interest to acquire a nuclear weapons capability because possessing such weapons would not increase national security, would not improve the stability of the regime, would not improve the prestige or status of the state, and would be detrimental to its economic development. Prevention can mainly, if not exclusively, be achieved through bilateral and multilateral negotiations in order to create the necessary geopolitical environment, including first of all appropriate security guarantees. To be most effective, preventive measures should be taken long before a crisis has arisen. We will not dwell further on this important facet.

Deterrence plays its role when a NNWS cannot be persuaded that acquiring a nuclear weapons capability is not in its best interest. In such a case it is essential for such a state to know, first, that any undeclared nuclear weapons program has a high probability of early detec-

---

Dr. Goldschmidt was deputy director general, head of the Department of Safeguards, International Atomic Energy Agency, May 1999–June 2005.

tion and, second, that if detected, extremely negative consequences would be inevitable (and not simply possible). Unfortunately, neither of these two deterrents is credibly in place today, and it is therefore essential to take the practical steps necessary to improve the situation.

For that, we need to draw on the lessons learned from previous nuclear proliferation crises.

Sensitive Fuel Cycle Activities

In the wake of the first Gulf War, when it was discovered that Saddam Hussein had secretly been developing nuclear weapons at undeclared sites, the International Atomic Energy Agency (IAEA) passed the 1997 Model Additional Protocol, designed to enable the agency to confirm there were no undeclared nuclear materials and activities in a NNWS. To date, however, 21 NNWS with known nuclear activities have no Additional Protocol in force; including at least three—Argentina, Brazil, and Iran—that are known to have uranium enrichment activities.

The international community should demand much more forcefully that such states sign and ratify the Additional Protocol, and the IAEA should mention these states explicitly in its annual report. The Nuclear Suppliers Group could also play a significant role in this respect by adopting a rule that no nuclear material, equipment, and know-how would be transferred to any country having conversion, enrichment, or reprocessing activities unless it has an Additional Protocol in force and unless these and all other nuclear facilities are covered by an INFCIRC/66-type safeguards agreement.[1]

Noncompliance

If a state has been found by the IAEA to be in noncompliance with its safeguards undertakings, experience with both North Korea and Iran has shown that, in order to conclude in a timely manner that there are

---

1 A comprehensive safeguards agreement remains in force only for so long as the state remains party to the NPT, whereas under a INFCIRC/66-type agreement, all nuclear material supplied or produced under that agreement would remain under safeguards, even if the state withdraws from the NPT, until such time as the IAEA has determined that such material is no longer subject to safeguards.

no undeclared nuclear material and activities in the state as a whole, the IAEA needs verification rights extending beyond those of the comprehensive safeguards agreements and Additional Protocol. This appears clearly from the director general's report of April 28, 2006, to the IAEA Board of Governors, where it is stated, "the Agency is unable to make progress in its efforts to provide assurance about the absence of undeclared nuclear material and activities in Iran," nor to assess "the role of the military in Iran's nuclear programme."

The report also states, "any progress in that regard requires . . . transparency that goes beyond the measures prescribed in the Safeguards Agreement and Additional Protocol."[2] A similar request was made in 2005 by both the director general and the Board of Governors. The problem here is that such IAEA board resolutions do not provide the agency with any additional legally binding verification authority. Therefore, the most effective and feasible way to establish the necessary authority is for the United Nations Security Council (UNSC) to adopt (under Chapter VII of the UN Charter) a generic (that is, not state specific) and legally binding resolution stating that if a state is reported by the IAEA to be in noncompliance:

- The noncompliant state will have to suspend all sensitive nuclear fuel cycle activities for a specified period of time,[3] but could by all means continue to produce electricity from nuclear power plants;

- If requested by the IAEA, the UNSC would automatically adopt a specific resolution (under Chapter VII) providing the IAEA additional verification authority until it is able to conclude that there are no undeclared nuclear materials and activities in the state and that its declarations to the agency are correct and complete; and

---

2 The April 28, 2006, report also states: "Additional transparency measures, including access to documentation, dual use equipment and relevant individuals, are, . . . still needed for the Agency to be able to verify the scope and nature of Iran's enrichment programme, the purpose and use of the dual use equipment and materials purchased by the PHRC [Iran's Physics Research Center], and the alleged studies which could have a military dimension."

3 This time would be at least until the IAEA has drawn the conclusion that the state declaration is correct and complete, or possibly longer, in line with what Director General ElBaradei has called a "rehabilitation period" or a "probation period, to build confidence again, before you can exercise your full rights." (See *Newsweek*, January 23, 2006.)

- No nuclear material shall henceforth be delivered to that state without the guarantee that all nuclear material and facilities declared to the IAEA would remain under IAEA's safeguards even if the state withdraws from the Nuclear Non-Proliferation Treaty (NPT).

As for the specific case of Iran, it is high time for the IAEA Board of Governors to formally request the UNSC to provide (under Chapter VII) the increased and legally binding investigation authority the agency has repeatedly stated is needed in Iran.

Withdrawal from the NPT

The current crisis in Iran appears to be a repetition of the earlier (and ongoing) crisis in North Korea.

North Korea
Every year since 1993, the IAEA has declared North Korea to be in noncompliance with its safeguards agreements and has reported North Korea to the UNSC, without the latter deciding to take any action. In 2003, North Korea gave notice that it was withdrawing from the NPT, and in 2004 it declared that it possessed nuclear weapons, without any move from the UNSC because China threatened to veto any resolution adverse to North Korea.

Iran
If the international community does not seem to have learned the lessons from the crisis in North Korea, Iran has. There are signs that it is preparing to follow the same steps as North Korea if the development of its nuclear program is threatened by the UNSC or any of its members.

Isn't Iran's deliberately provocative attitude a step toward preparing for its withdrawal from the NPT, as is its letter of March 21, 2006, addressed to Secretary General Kofi Annan that complained about the fact that senior U.S. officials have publicly threatened to resort to force against Iran "in total contempt of international law and the fundamental principles of the Charter of the United Nations"?

Also, on May 7, 2006, the Iranian Parliament, in a letter to Secretary General Kofi Annan, threatened to force Iran's government to withdraw from the NPT if pressure continues on Tehran to suspend uranium enrichment activities.

It is therefore essential for the international community not to wait for Iran's withdrawal from the NPT, but for the UNSC to adopt (under Chapter VII of the UN Charter) a generic and legally binding resolution stating that if a state withdraws from the NPT after being found by the IAEA to be in noncompliance with its safeguards undertakings:

- Such withdrawal constitutes a threat to international peace and security as defined under Article 39 of the UN Charter; and
- All materials and equipment made available to such a state, or resulting from the assistance provided to it under a comprehensive safeguards agreement, will be forthwith removed from that state under IAEA supervision and remain under the agency's safeguards.

Conclusion

The longer the UNSC takes to adopt the resolutions suggested in this paper, the more difficult it will be to save the credibility of the nonproliferation regime.

President Kennedy predicted in the early 1960s that before the end of the following decade there would be between 20 and 25 states possessing nuclear weapons. Fortunately, this did not materialize, but many changes have occurred since then. Today, inaction may lead to Kennedy's prediction coming true, with dreadful consequences for international security, particularly if one takes into account the new dimension of international terrorism. Einstein once said, "The world will not be destroyed by those who do evil, but by those who let them do and refuse to intervene."